REVISE EDEXCEL GCSE
Business

Units 1, 3 and 5

REVISION GUIDE

Series Consultant: Harry Smith

Authors: Rob Jones and Andrew Redfern

Contributions by Dave Gray

A note from the publisher

In order to ensure that this resource offers high-quality support for the associated Pearson qualification, it has been through a review process by the awarding body. This process confirms that this resource fully covers the teaching and learning content of the specification or part of a specification at which it is aimed. It also confirms that it demonstrates an appropriate balance between the development of subject skills, knowledge and understanding, in addition to preparation for assessment.

Endorsement does not cover any guidance on assessment activities or processes (e.g. practice questions or advice on how to answer assessment questions), included in the resource nor does it prescribe any particular approach to the teaching or delivery of a related course.

While the publishers have made every attempt to ensure that advice on the qualification and its assessment is accurate, the official specification and associated assessment guidance materials are the only authoritative source of information and should always be referred to for definitive guidance.

Pearson examiners have not contributed to any sections in this resource relevant to examination papers for which they have responsibility.

Examiners will not use endorsed resources as a source of material for any assessment set by Pearson.

Endorsement of a resource does not mean that the resource is required to achieve this Pearson qualification, nor does it mean that it is the only suitable material available to support the qualification, and any resource lists produced by the awarding body shall include this and other appropriate resources.

ALWAYS LEARNING

PEARSON

Contents

This book covers the GCSE Business Studies and GCSE Business Studies and Economics pathways. If you are studying:

GCSE Business Studies – you should work through **Unit 1** and **Unit 3**

GCSE Business Studies and Economics – you should work through **Unit 1** and **Unit 5**

GCSE Business Studies (Short Course) – you should work through **Unit 1**.

A small bit of small print

Edexcel publishes Sample Assessment Material and the Specification on its website. This is the official content and this book should be used in conjunction with it. The questions in Now try this have been written to help you practise every topic in the book. Remember: the real exam questions may not look like this.

Target grade ranges

Target grade ranges are quoted in this book for some of the questions. Students targeting this grade range should be aiming to get most of the marks available. Students targeting a higher grade should be aiming to get all of the marks available.

1-to-1
page match with the
Revision
Workbook
ISBN 9781446903766

Businesses

A BUSINESS is an organisation whose PURPOSE is to produce goods and services to meet the needs of customers. A business might produce its own goods or buy them from a SUPPLIER and sell them to CUSTOMERS.

Things to think about when setting up a business:
- ☑ Is there a business opportunity?
- ☑ How will the business be financed?
- ☑ What is required to get the business up and running?
- ☑ What legal aspects have to be considered?
- ☑ What products or services will be sold and to whom?

What businesses do

SUPPLIERS   PRODUCTION   CUSTOMERS / CONSUMERS

BUY FROM ⟸   BUSINESS   ⟹ SELL TO

Supplier: A business that sells (supplies) products to another business.

Production: Using raw materials, labour and machinery to make products.

Customer: A person or organisation that buys the product or service.
Consumer: The person that uses (consumes) the product.

The market is where buyers and sellers meet to exchange goods and services.

Worked example

target **F-E**

What is the purpose of a business? Select **one** answer.   **(1 mark)**
A ☐ To give everyone a job
B ☐ To make big profits for its owners
C ☒ To provide goods and services
D ☐ To pay taxes to the government

Each option in this question is something that a business will do or hope to do, but C is the actual **purpose** of a business.

Now try this

1 Which of the following is most likely to be a supplier to a small business making costumes for parties? Select **one** answer.   **(1 mark)**

target **G-F**

A ☐ A clown who entertains children at parties
B ☐ A manufacturer of buttons
C ☐ A taxi that takes people to parties
D ☐ People who buy costumes

Understanding customer needs 1

Most customer needs are based on good quality, good product range, convenient location, good customer service and a fair price. The problem is that all customers are different and need different things!

Market research

Market research can tell a business:
- ✓ what features customers want
- ✓ how much they are willing to pay
- ✓ where they shop
- ✓ what age and gender they are
- ✓ who the main competitors are
- ✓ if the market is growing or shrinking.

These questions can be answered through:
- PRIMARY RESEARCH – collecting data that did not exist before (e.g. by asking questions).
- SECONDARY RESEARCH – collecting data that already exists (e.g. internet research).

Worked example

target
D-C

Lisa Gallagher believes there is a growing market for gardening services. She has conducted some market research to test her idea and has summarised her findings.

Type of household	Percentage
Single – no children	7
Single – with children	11
Single – pensioner	28
Couple – no children	9
Couple – with children	31
Couple – pensioners	14

Table 1

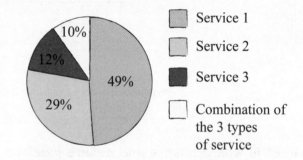

- Service 1
- Service 2
- Service 3
- Combination of the 3 types of service

10% 12% 49% 29%

Figure 1

Study Table 1 and Figure 1. According to this information, which three conclusions can Lisa draw from the data? Select **three** answers. **(3 marks)**

A ☒ 100% more single pensioners than pensioner couples are interested in Lisa's business

B ☐ Lisa should not offer Services 2 or 3 as there is no demand

C ☒ Her main two segments are couples with children and single pensioners

D ☒ More than half of people prefer something other than Service 1

E ☐ Couples with children are more likely to use Service 1

EXAM ALERT!

Fewer than four in ten students got all three marks for this question. When interpreting data in figures and tables, be prepared to make comparisons, carry out calculations, identify characteristics and look at trends.

This was a real exam question that a lot of students struggled with – **be prepared!**

ResultsPlus

Now try this

target
G-F

1 Which **one** of the following is an example of primary market research? Select **one** answer. **(1 mark)**

A ☐ Government statistics   C ☐ Survey of customers

B ☐ Newspaper articles   D ☐ Internet research

Understanding customer needs 2

PRIMARY RESEARCH (field research) is collecting information that did not exist before. This first-hand contact with customers is valuable to a business in understanding their market.

SECONDARY RESEARCH (desk research) is the process of gathering secondary data, which is information that already exists.

Surveys — Focus groups — Observations

Primary research

Questionnaires — Experiments

- More accurate.
- Up to date.
- Specific to needs.
- Effective at collecting qualitative data.
- Direct customer contact.

Sales data — Internet sites — Local newspapers

Secondary research

Telephone directories — Market reports — Government statistics

- More general.
- Less time-consuming.
- Effective at collecting quantitative data.

Qualitative and quantitative data

- QUALITATIVE DATA – information about opinions, judgements and attitudes.
- QUANTITATIVE DATA – data that can be expressed as numbers and statistically analysed.

When INTERPRETING DATA, businesses should look for issues to identify the potential size of the market, trends in the market (e.g. tastes) and an indication of what customers want.

Worked example

target D-C

Which of the following are the benefits of conducting secondary market research instead of primary market research? Select **two** answers.   **(2 marks)**

A ☐ It adds value to products

B ☒ It is less time-consuming

C ☒ It offers a wider range of information

D ☐ It is more specific to the target market

E ☐ It will lower the costs of production

B and C are the only two **benefits** of secondary research over primary research.

Now try this

target E-D

1 Which of the following would **not** be an appropriate method of market research for a new small business? Select **one** answer.   **(1 mark)**

A ☐ Employing a specialist market research company to carry out a survey of 10 000 people

B ☐ Using published statistics about market trends

C ☐ Asking customers to fill in a short questionnaire on the premises

D ☐ Conducting an interview with a group of volunteer customers

3

Market mapping

MARKET MAPPING helps businesses to identify market segments and position their products through identifying gaps in the market.

Analysing customer buying habits

Businesses must research potential customers' buying preferences, i.e. who the customers are, what they want, what they buy and how often they buy. Businesses can do this through:

- finding information about customers
- using their own experience
- looking at existing businesses and trying competitors' products
- observation and surveys.

Market segments

A MARKET SEGMENT is a group of buyers with similar characteristics and buying habits. A market can be segmented in many ways:

- Age (e.g. 18–24).
- Gender (e.g. male).
- Income (e.g. socio-economic group).
- Lifestyle (e.g. adventure).
- Life-stage (e.g. newlyweds).

Market segmentation

Segmentation allows a business to:

- meet specific customer needs
- differentiate their products
- focus on a specific group of customers
- target marketing activity
- develop a unique brand image
- build close customer relationships.

Example of a market map using price and quality.

A MARKET MAPPING diagram can be used to position and compare products in a market, and identify opportunities where customer needs are not being met.

---

target
E-D

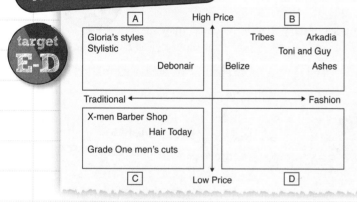

According to the market map, where is there a gap in the market? **(1 mark)**

A business that provides:

A ☐ high price / traditional

B ☐ high price / fashion

C ☐ low price / traditional

D ☒ low price / fashion

Option D is the only quadrant where there are no other businesses.

---

target
C-B

1. Which **two** of the following are **most likely** to be important in spotting a new business opportunity in the cycling market? Select **two** answers. **(2 marks)**

   A ☐ Being able to produce a product cheaply

   B ☐ Recognising a new gap in the market

   C ☐ Being a keen cyclist

   D ☐ Identifying the possible competitors

   E ☐ Having a large amount of personal savings

Competition

A business might use a number of criteria to analyse and judge the STRENGTHS and WEAKNESSES of its potential COMPETITION in order to improve its 'business offering' and DIFFERENTIATE from them.

Wider product range

Better after-sales service

Stronger brand image

More enjoyable experience

Ways to compete

Better product features

Better design

Higher quality

Instead of competing head-to-head, businesses can try to DIFFERENTIATE their products.

Head-to-Head Competition

| BUSINESS | PRICE > < PRICE | COMPETITOR |

DIFFERENTIATION

QUALITY

| BUSINESS | | COMPETITOR |

CUSTOMER SERVICE

Branding

A brand is a named product that customers see as being different from other products, and that they can associate or identify with. A company or product can develop a unique brand image that customers associate them with.

Worked example

target D-C

Sam is a driving instructor.

Which **two** of the following methods are most likely to give Sam a competitive advantage? Select **two** answers. **(2 marks)**

A ☒ Providing high-quality tuition   D ☐ Operating in a competitive market

B ☐ Operating as a sole trader   E ☐ Providing a service for the community

C ☒ Providing a personalised service

> A and C are ways in which a business can differentiate what it does.

Now try this

JayCD is a small independent music store operating on narrow profit margins. It is facing strong competition from a local supermarket, which sells chart CDs at very low prices.

1 Which **two** are the most likely methods JayCD might use to compete with the supermarket? Select **two** answers. **(2 marks)**

target D-C

A ☐ Lower its prices below that of the supermarket

B ☐ Launch an advertising campaign on national television

C ☐ Provide an ordering service for hard-to-find CDs for their customers

D ☐ Open up two new stores in the town

E ☐ Focus on improving the quality of customer service

Added value 1

ADDED VALUE is the increased worth that a business creates for a product; it is the difference between what a business pays its suppliers and the price that it is able to charge for the product.

A simple idea?

Basically, a business can add value to its product by lowering costs or adding something that will make customers willing to pay a higher price.

Adding value is very closely linked to profit.

More convenience

Unique selling point

Greater speed of service ——— **Ways to add value** ——— Better design

Branding

Improved quality

Adding value

£100	£30 Value added: what the business adds
Price	£70 Variable cost

Worked example

 target C-B

Sparkle Oven Cleaning Company Ltd is a business offering an oven cleaning service. Eddie Lowe, the owner, aims to provide an exceptional cleaning service. Eddie says that the focus of the business is on competitive prices, high standards and good customer service.

B and E are things that customers would be willing to pay more for. Option B would provide a better all-round service, and Option E would improve convenience. The other three options might improve his business but would not **add value**.

Which **two** of the following might be the best ways in which Eddie could add value to his business?
Select **two** answers.   **(2 marks)**

A ☐ Employing an accountant to manage his cash flow

B ☒ Offering free after-care visits to check customer satisfaction

C ☐ Making sure that he has an excellent relationship with his bank

D ☐ Buying a van with the name of the company clearly written on the side

E ☒ Providing a weekend service so that customers do not need time off work

Now try this

target C-B

Mark Steel is a qualified hairdresser looking to set up in business as a sole trader.

1   Which **two** of the following are sources of added value for Mark's business?
Select **two** answers.   **(2 marks)**

A ☐ Offering late-night opening appointments

B ☐ Asking customers to complete a questionnaire after their appointment

C ☐ Ensuring he manages cash flow effectively

D ☐ Providing free refreshments and drinks for customers

E ☐ Locating in an area where other hairdressers already operate

Added value 2

Adding value is important to a business for a number of reasons. A business must decide how best to combine the features of its products to add value.

The importance of added value

The added value of a product goes towards paying off a company's costs. The higher the added value, the sooner costs can be paid off and the quicker a business will make a profit. The more value a business can add to its products, the more chance the business has of success, survival and long-term growth.

Unique selling point (USP)

A USP is one another way to add value to a product. A USP will also help a business compete.

Developing a USP can be aided through understanding customer needs and market mapping.

Mix and match

Most products combine a range of features to add value and improve competitiveness. The most successful products are the ones that are able to keep costs down as they add new features or benefits.

Unique combination of ingredients

Freshly handmade

Friendly service

Free drink with every sandwich

Organic bread

Worked example

target C–B

Lisa Gallagher believes there is a growing market for gardening services.

Which **two** of the following are strategies that Lisa might use to help her business achieve high levels of added value?
Select **two** answers.   **(2 marks)**

A ☐ Ensure a profit is made on every job completed

B ☐ Give price discounts

C ☒ Visit every customer 48 hours after work is completed to take feedback

D ☒ Develop a strong brand awareness in the local area

E ☐ Compare the prices of Lisa's competitors every month

Option C will add value through raising after-sales service, and Option D will add value through a stronger brand image. Customers are willing to pay more for these things.

Now try this

target C–B

1 Which of the following is most likely to be a reason why a business would try to add value to its products? Select **one** answer.   **(1 mark)**

A ☐ To increase the materials it buys

B ☐ To add a USP

C ☐ To differentiate its product

D ☐ To improve its chances of survival in the long term

7

Franchising 1

A FRANCHISE is the right given by one business to other businesses to sell goods or services using its name. The businesses that buy into a franchise remain as independent businesses.

Who's who?

- FRANCHISOR – the business that gives franchisees the right to sell its product or service.
- FRANCHISEE – a business that agrees to manufacture, distribute or provide a branded product, under licence by a franchisor.

The principle of franchising

The principle behind a franchise is the expansion of an established business through licensing the right for ENTREPRENEURS to set up their own business using the name, equipment and products of the franchise in return for a fee or share of the sales revenue.

What does the franchisee get when they buy a franchise?

A franchise is like buying a ready-made business in a box!

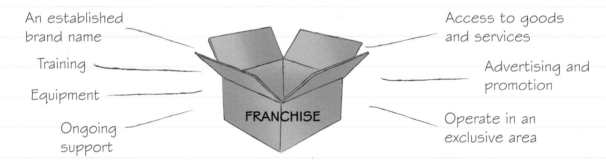

An established brand name

Training

Equipment

Ongoing support

FRANCHISE

Access to goods and services

Advertising and promotion

Operate in an exclusive area

Worked example

target **E-D**

What type of organisation is set up 'under licence' to use an established business name?

Select **one** answer. **(1 mark)**

A ☐ Sole trader

B ☐ Enterprise

C ☒ Franchise

D ☐ Private limited company

The answer is C because a franchise is the only type of business that allows through licensing the right for others to 'buy into' the business and set up the business under the franchisor's name.

Now try this

target **C-B**

1 Which **two** of the following are correct statements about a franchise? Select **two** answers. **(2 marks)**

A ☐ A franchisee can use the name of the franchise in advertising

B ☐ The franchisee gives the franchisor the right to sell its product

C ☐ A franchise is public limited company

D ☐ Only two businesses are part of a franchise

E ☐ A franchise is the right given by one business to another to sell its products

Franchising 2

There are benefits for a new business setting up as a franchise compared to setting up as a sole trader. However, there are also drawbacks.

Brand image / reputation already established

Access to tried-and-tested products

Possibly an established customer base

Higher chance of survival

Expensive marketing costs covered by the franchise

Benefits of a franchise

Specific support and training provided

Drawbacks of a franchise

- Start-up costs can be expensive.
- Royalty payments.
- Complicated application process.
- Lack of autonomy and control.
- Limited flexibility to make your own decisions.

Location

For some small businesses, such as a retail shop or restaurant, location is vital. But for others, location is less important. Factors in choosing a location might include:

Proximity to competition

Busy (passing trade)

Access (parking, etc.)

Cost

Worked example

target D-C

Identify **two** possible disadvantages of operating the business as a franchise. Select **two** answers. **(2 marks)**

A ☒ The cost of the initial investment can be high

B ☐ Franchises have to take out a patent

C ☐ Franchises have to pay a higher rate of Value Added Tax (VAT)

D ☒ There is a lack of freedom for the owner in making decisions

E ☐ It can access help and advice from the franchise owner

EXAM ALERT!

Just over half of students got both marks for this question. Options A and D are the only two answers that could be a disadvantage.

This was a real exam question that a lot of students struggled with – **be prepared!**

ResultsPlus

When completing multiple-choice questions, underline the command words in the question. In this case, 'two' and 'disadvantages'. This will ensure you know exactly what the question wants you to do.

Now try this

target C-B

1   Which **two** of the following are possible advantages to an individual of starting a business as a franchise rather than as a sole trader? Select **two** answers. **(2 marks)**

A ☐ The franchisor pays the franchisee to set up the business

B ☐ Franchises pay lower rates of Value Added Tax than a sole trader

C ☐ A franchise is likely to be an established business

D ☐ The franchisee has complete freedom to make their own decisions

E ☐ The franchisee can benefit from national advertising of the franchise

Enterprise

ENTERPRISE is a word often used in business, which represents the ideas and initiatives involved in starting a new business. Businesses might supply a GOOD (physical and tangible product such as a car) or a SERVICE (a non-physical, intangible product such as insurance).

Entrepreneurs, enterprise and enterprises

Entrepreneur – a person who owns and runs their own business and takes risks.

Enterprise – the initial spark and idea for a business and the willingness by an individual to show initiative, take a risk and undertake a new venture.

Enterprises – another word used for businesses.

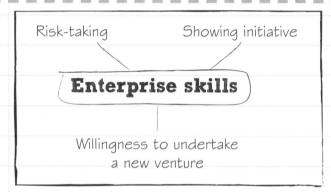

Risk-taking   Showing initiative

Enterprise skills

Willingness to undertake a new venture

The importance of risk

Entrepreneurs take risks when they start their own business. There is a chance that their businesses will not survive and therefore they risk their own time, livelihood and money. Enterprise is important because new businesses create jobs and wealth in the economy.

Worked example

target G–F

Which **two** of the following are key features of enterprise?
Select **two** answers.   **(2 marks)**

A ☐ Employing at least one worker

B ☐ Having the right qualifications to run a business

C ☒ Being prepared to take risks

D ☒ Having a willingness to take on a new venture

E ☐ Registering as a private limited company

C and D are the correct answers. When answering questions about enterprise, remember that it involves the things required to start a new business.

Now try this

target G–F

1 Which **two** of the following are key enterprise skills?
Select **two** answers.   **(2 marks)**

A ☐ A willingness to take risks

B ☐ A willingness to employ at least five workers

C ☐ A willingness to take the initiative

D ☐ A willingness to follow a course of study in business

E ☐ The ability to raise finance

Thinking creatively

The success of many businesses depends on the ability of the owners to come up with new, unique and creative ideas, in order to compete, to identify new opportunities and to differentiate themselves from competitors.

Better products

Considers 'What if?' questions

Unique ideas and products

Cheaper production techniques

Thinking creatively

Identify new opportunities and markets

Improved customer service

DELIBERATE CREATIVITY is the intentional creation of new ideas through recognised and accepted techniques. For example:

- creating lists
- mind mapping / brainstorming
- make it bigger / smaller
- combining things together.

Blue skies and lateral thinking

- BLUE SKIES THINKING is coming up with as many ideas as possible to solve a problem.
- LATERAL THINKING involves thinking differently to try to find new and unexpected ideas. DE BONO'S SIX THINKING HATS is an example of lateral thinking.

De Bono's six thinking hats give six different ways to think about an issue, idea or problem.

Facts about an idea

Thinking about what they are thinking

Emotions are gut feelings about an idea

How to get around a problem creatively

Difficulties of the idea

Positive aspects of the idea

Worked example

target B-A

Deliberate creativity involves which **two** of the following techniques? Select **two** answers.   (2 marks)

A ☐ Starting a business that provides a service

B ☒ Brainstorming business ideas

C ☒ Creating lists to compare options

D ☐ Producing a cash-flow forecast

E ☐ Preparing a business plan

EXAM ALERT!

Four in ten students got both marks for this question. Deliberate creativity involves developing ideas through recognised techniques such as brainstorming (B) and creating lists (C).

This was a real exam question that a lot of students struggled with – **be prepared!**   ResultsPlus

Now try this

target C-B

Vakas Shah used his engineering background to develop CycleSure, a lightweight but strong cable that secures the wheels and frame of a bicycle.

1   Vakas needed to think creatively to produce CycleSure. Why is thinking creatively important? Select **one** answer.   (1 mark)

A ☐ Avoids having to answer the 'what if?' question   C ☐ Generates competitive advantage

B ☐ Increases the calculated risk   D ☐ Avoids the need for lateral thinking

Questions entrepreneurs ask

It is vitally important that entrepreneurs ask themselves questions when they start their own business.

Helps identify business objectives

Helps develop aspects of the business plan

Why ask questions?

Helps make important decisions

Identifies potential problems and pitfalls

Why? and Why not?

These sorts of questions will help identify the purpose and direction of the business.

- Why do I want to start my own business?
- Why do I want to change?
- Why not set up my own website business?

How? Where? and When?

These questions help identify specifics about the business that can help form parts of the business plan.

- How do I set up the business?
- How do I build up a customer base?
- How will I research my market?
- Where can I get help and advice?
- When could I open the business?

What if?

These questions allow an entrepreneur to assess the value and likelihood of any possible outcome. Solutions can then be identified from these questions.

- What if my business loses money?
- What if my customers do not like my products?
- What if there is too much competition?
- What if I am ill for a long period of time?

Worked example

target D–C

Alyssa has started a singing career. She needs to buy PA equipment and a microphone.

Which **two** of the following questions would she be most likely to ask to help her buy the most suitable products? Select **two** answers.   **(2 marks)**

A ☐ Where are the locations she will be singing?

B ☐ When will she need to buy the equipment?

C ☒ What does she have to spend?

D ☐ Where does she live?

E ☒ What space for equipment does she have in her van?

Consider what questions will give Alyssa information about the size, power, cost and other features of the equipment. These are more likely to be 'What' than 'Where' or 'When' questions.

Now try this

target G–F

John runs a sports shop in Norwich. He is going to advertise his new range of trainers in the local paper over the summer months.

1   Which of the following questions would he ask? Select **one** answer.   **(1 mark)**

A ☐ What if his staff take holidays in summer?

B ☐ What if local people go abroad in summer?

C ☐ What if he needs to change his store layout in summer?

D ☐ What if he redecorates the shop in summer?

Invention and innovation

RESEARCH AND DEVELOPMENT → INVENTION → POTENTIAL PRODUCTS AND PROCESSES → INNOVATION → PRODUCTS READY TO SELL TO CUSTOMERS

Risk

Invention and innovation are risky. They can be expensive and time consuming, and many new products fail to make it to market. Businesses gain a competitive advantage from invention and innovation, but some businesses choose to wait to copy or 'follow' other businesses, creating 'me too' products.

Protecting business ideas

- PATENTS – right of ownership of an invention, design or process when it is registered with the government.
- COPYRIGHT – legal ownership of material such as books, music and films which prevent these being copied by others.
- TRADEMARKS – the logo, symbol, sign, or other features of a product or business that cannot be copied by others.

Worked example

target D-C

Which **one** of the following best describes the term 'invention'? Select **one** answer. (1 mark)

A ☒ Identifying new products and new ways of making products

B ☐ Identifying a gap in the market for new products

C ☐ New business ideas which are profitable

D ☐ The process of transforming new ideas into products that can be sold

EXAM ALERT!

One in three students got this question right. On topics where there are similarities between key terms, try to remember one key difference to help you distinguish between them. In this case, innovation takes invention one step further to create actual products for consumers.

This was a real exam question that a lot of students struggled with – **be prepared!** ResultsPlus

Now try this

target D-C

1 What is **one** possible benefit of a patent to the patent owner? Select **one** answer. (1 mark)

A ☐ Prevents another business from using the same brand name

B ☐ Provides the right of ownership of an invention or process

C ☐ Is an insurance policy which provides protection from financial loss

D ☐ Ensures the business will not make a loss for 20 years

Taking a calculated risk

Taking a CALCULATED RISK is about putting a numerical value or probability on a risk and the likelihood of it coming true. Weighing up the risks and rewards of a new business idea is important in judging the outcome and viability of a start-up.

Calculated risk

A business can calculate risk through market research, and understanding the risk can help a business make decisions that will reduce the likelihood of a negative outcome. Examples of calculated risk include:

- 50:50 chance of an advert's success
- 1 in 3 chance of a business failing
- 10% of customers will return products.

Making mistakes

Reducing risk is an important part of running a business, but entrepreneurs often have to fail before they learn how to be successful. Making mistakes is an important part of developing a business. As entrepreneurs learn from their mistakes they will become better at calculating risk.

Risk can be calculated by identifying and comparing UPSIDES and DOWNSIDES. Upsides are things that can go right (or the reward). Downsides are the things that can go wrong. Below is an example of the upsides and downsides of selling products through a website instead of in-store (scoring out of 5).

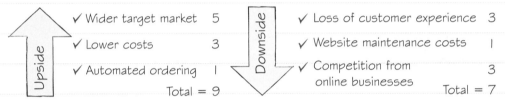

Upside
- ✓ Wider target market   5
- ✓ Lower costs   3
- ✓ Automated ordering   1

Total = 9

Downside
- ✓ Loss of customer experience   3
- ✓ Website maintenance costs   1
- ✓ Competition from online businesses   3

Total = 7

Worked example

Sonia Fletcher set up as a sole trader selling cakes made from organic ingredients.

Which **one** of the following is an example of a calculated risk for Sonia's business?
Select **one** answer.

- A ☐ Sonia's costs had risen by 30% in the past 6 months
- B ☐ Sonia has calculated her yearly income tax as £795
- C ☒ There is an 80:20 chance of Sonia's business failing
- D ☐ Sonia has estimated that demand will rise by 10% over the next six months

EXAM ALERT!

Six in ten students got this right. C is the only answer that gives a numerical value to a risk.

This was a real exam question that a lot of students struggled with – **be prepared!**

Now try this

Marcus Borega is a sole trader. His business imports high-quality cars from the USA.

1   Which **one** of the following is an example of a calculated risk for Marcus?
Select **one** answer.   **(1 mark)**

- A ☐ His fixed costs are 50% of his total costs
- B ☐ There is a 40% chance of the business surviving the first year
- C ☐ Marcus' variable costs rise by 25% in the first six months
- D ☐ 10% of his customers will be over 65 years of age

Other important enterprise skills

Being a successful entrepreneur is about more than just taking risks and identifying an opportunity. There is a range of important skills that also contribute to an individual's success.

Planning – identifying a direction and plan of action for the business.

Drive – being hardworking and motivated to achieve success.

Thinking ahead – having the foresight to identify potential problems.

Determination – being resilient when things go wrong / not giving up.

Seeing opportunities – having the creativity and imagination to do things differently.

Use this mnemonic to remember the important enterprise skills: Please Don't Trip Down Stairs

Mind maps

Mind maps are often used in 'Blue Skies Thinking' (see page 11). Mind maps are also useful in helping an entrepreneur get their ideas down on paper when thinking ahead, planning the business and trying to identify new opportunities. A mind map to remember the marketing mix might look like this:

Marketing mix

- Product
  - Specifications
  - Design
  - Packaging
  - Function
- Price
  - Premium (high)
  - Discounted (low)
  - Price match (same)
- Promotion
  - Advertising
  - PR brochures
  - Direct mail
  - Sales promotions
- Place
  - Direct / Online
  - Retailer
  - Wholesaler

Worked example

target **C-B**

> Alex Tew took 20 minutes to come up with a successful business idea. Within three months he had made a million dollars by selling pixels on a website to businesses. The businesses could buy any number of pixels for $1 each and use them to place an advert link to their business.

Which **one** of the following enterprise skills do you think was the **most** important in contributing to Alex's success? Select **one** answer.   **(1 mark)**

A ☐ He asked why people would pay $1 for a pixel on a website

B ☐ He showed initiative in solving his problem of student debt

C ☒ He didn't just ask all the right questions, he actually got up and did it

D ☐ He thought creatively about ways to make a million

The correct answer is C because actually setting up and running the business not only shows drive and determination, but also the willingness to take a risk. Initiative (B) and creativity (D) are both important enterprise skills, but perhaps not as important as C in Alex's case. Always think carefully if the question asks you to identify the 'most important' issue.

Now try this

target **E-D**

1 Successful entrepreneurs need to think creatively and make connections between ideas. What is the name of the diagram which can be used to record words and ideas connected to a central word or idea?

Select **one** answer.   **(1 mark)**

A ☐ Spreadsheet   C ☐ Scatter diagram

B ☐ Market map   D ☐ Mind map

Objectives when starting up

All businesses set OBJECTIVES. Sometimes these are financial objectives, which can be expressed in money terms. Businesses also have non-financial objectives. These are more personal and may involve helping others.

Objectives

Objectives are the goals that a business is trying to achieve. Objectives are important for all businesses, especially business start-ups. Setting objectives gives a business a direction and a target to measure success against. Businesses do not all have the same objectives, some of these can be personal to the entrepreneur.

Often businesses set more than one objective, which may include:

- financial aspects
- non-financial aspects.

When deciding the best objectives for a business, consider the type of business, the characteristics of the entrepreneur and how competitive the industry is. A start-up will often have more modest objectives than a large business.

Typical objectives for a start-up

Financial objectives

- Survival
- Profit and income
- Wealth
- Financial security

Non-financial objectives

- Personal satisfaction
- Independence and control
- Helping others (social enterprise)

Worked example

Both Option A and Option E are examples of non-financial objectives. Option A involves helping others, while Option E is about independence and control (being your own boss). Options B–D are not really viable objectives for starting a business.

target F-E

Which **two** of the following are the most likely reasons why an individual would want to start a business? Select **two** answers.   **(2 marks)**

A ☒ To use the profits of a business to make a difference

B ☐ To work fewer hours each week

C ☐ To avoid paying income tax

D ☐ To show their boss that they are as good as them

E ☒ To control their own future

Now try this

1 Which **three** of the following are the most likely reasons why Sonia decided to set up as a sole trader?
Select **three** answers.   **(3 marks)**

A ☐ She will benefit from limited liability

B ☐ She could raise finance from selling shares

C ☐ To have greater control within the business

D ☐ She would take all of the profits

E ☐ She would have the ability to make her own decisions

F ☐ It would make survival easier

Qualities shown by entrepreneurs

Successful entrepreneurs have a number of important qualities. There is no definitive list of qualities that make the perfect entrepreneur. Each entrepreneur will have his or her own mix of qualities that make them successful in business.

Entrepreneurial qualities

Quality	Example
Planning	Identifying a direction and plan of action for the business, e.g. deciding to buy a new machine in a year when new technology will be available.
Initiative	Being pro-active and getting a job done, e.g. approaching a competitor to discuss the possibility of working together on a new product.
Taking risks	Entrepreneurs are risk takers because they invest their own time and capital, e.g. ordering 20% more stock in the hope that sales will increase shortly.
Determination	Being resilient when things go wrong / not giving up, e.g. working into the evening to solve a problem.
Making decisions	Entrepreneurs need good judgement, e.g. deciding the most suitable source of start-up finding.
Persuasion	Being able to convince customers, suppliers and banks, e.g. talking a supplier round to give an extra 2% discount on an order.
Leadership	Entrepreneurs employ and lead others, e.g. motivating staff to meet a deadline.
Luck	Sometimes luck counts, e.g. an ice cream manufacturer has its best sales because of the hottest summer on record.

> In reality there are many other qualities that entrepreneurs value. When analysing a case study, consider which are the most relevant for that entrepreneur and think of specific examples where the quality might be needed.

Worked example

target
C-B

Match the qualities on the left with the examples on the right.   (4 marks)

Quality			Example
Leadership	i	a	Reorganising the layout of the factory
Determination	ii	b	Talking a worker around to doing some overtime
Making decisions	iii	c	Having been rejected for a loan by four banks, applying to another bank for the loan
Persuasion	iv	d	Having a vision for where the business should be in two years time

This question asks you to match up entrepreneurial qualities with an example. You need to be ready for 'match up' questions. This is why it is very important to revise key terms. There are often key terms that are very similar (e.g. invention and innovation) so be careful and ensure that you are certain before moving on.

Now try this

target
E-D

1   Which **two** of the following are key qualities needed by an entrepreneur?
Select **two** answers.   (2 marks)

A ☐ A willingness to take risks   D ☐ A degree in Business Studies

B ☐ A willingness to employ at least   E ☐ The ability to raise finance
five workers

C ☐ A willingness to take the initiative

Revenues, costs and profits 1

A business must understand the difference between the price it charges to customers and the cost of producing its products. If it knows how many products it sells, it can calculate its total revenue and its total costs. It can then calculate profit.

REVENUE, SALES REVENUE or TURNOVER is the amount of income received from selling goods or services over a period of time.

Price × Quantity = Total revenue

 £ × = TR

- FIXED COSTS do not vary with the output produced by a business, e.g. salaries and business rates.
- VARIABLE COSTS change directly with the number of products made, e.g. raw materials and labour.

Variable costs = Cost of one unit × Quantity produced

Total costs

TOTAL COSTS are all the costs of a business.

It can be calculated using the formula:

Fixed costs + Variable costs = Total costs

i.e. £400 + (£5 × 100) = £400 + £500 = £900

 + = TC

Worked example

 target **D-C**

Hancock's is a small pottery business which specialises in garden plant pots. It has the following financial information for one month.

Number of pots produced and sold: 150
Average price per pot: £10
Variable costs per pot: £2
Fixed costs per month: £500

What are the total costs for Hancock's during the month?
Select **one** answer.   **(1 mark)**

A ☐ £450   C ☒ £800

B ☐ £650   D ☐ £1500

EXAM ALERT!

Just over half of students got this question right. Just because some of the figures in the options given can be arrived at, it doesn't mean this is the right option.

Total costs = fixed costs + variable costs.

This was a real exam question that a lot of students struggled with – **be prepared!**

 ResultsPlus

Now try this

 target **B-A**

1 The following table shows the costs, revenues and profits for Merry Maids for a two-month period.

Fill in the **four** blanks (a)–(d) to complete the table.   **(4 marks)**

	October	November
Total receipts	£14 000	£12 000
Fixed costs	£2000	£2000
Variable costs	(a)	(c)
Total costs	£9000	(d)
Profit	(b)	£5000

Revenues, costs and profits 2

A business must be able to calculate whether it is making a profit or loss. It must also understand how making a profit or loss can have an impact on the business and its owners.

Profit and loss

PROFIT occurs when revenues of a business are greater than its total costs. If a business's costs are greater than its revenues then it will make a LOSS. Profit or loss can be calculated used the formula:

Total revenue – Total costs = Profit or Loss

i.e. £1000 – £900 = £100 profit

 = PROFIT or LOSS

Profit is the objective of many businesses because it allows a business to:
- ☑ survive
- ☑ reinvest profits for expansion
- ☑ give an incentive to start the business
- ☑ provide security and savings
- ☑ reward employees
- ☑ generate wealth for the owner.

Ways to increase profits

- ☑ Lower variable costs.
- ☑ Lower fixed costs.
- ☑ Increase the sales price.
- ☑ Increase the quantity of sales.

Making a loss can have a significant impact on a business. The business might be:
- unable to repay loans
- unable to pay bills such as wages
- experiencing cash-flow problems
- unable to survive, leading to the business stopping trading.

Worked example

target
A–A*

The owners of Hancock's decide to try to increase profit.

Which **three** of the actions below will most likely achieve this, assuming it sells the same number of pots each month?
Select **three** answers.   **(3 marks)**

A ☒ Buy cheaper raw materials to make its products

B ☒ Increase the sales price of an average pot to £11

C ☐ Increase the number of workers employed over the weekend

D ☐ Buy more expensive raw materials to make its pots

E ☐ Increase advertising expenditure

F ☒ Relocate to cheaper premises

EXAM ALERT!

Fewer than six in ten students got all three marks for this question. Options A, B and F are all correct answers because each would either raise revenue (B) or lower costs (A and F).

This was a real exam question that a lot of students struggled with – **be prepared!**

ResultsPlus

Now try this

target
B–A

A business spent:
- £10 000 on raw materials
- £30 000 on fixed costs
- £7500 on other variable costs and had a turnover of £50 000

1 The business now buys its raw materials 10% more cheaply from a new supplier. What effect will this have on profit?
Select **one** answer.   **(1 mark)**

The profit level will:

A ☐ Increase by £2500

B ☐ Fall by £2500

C ☐ Increase from £2500 to £3500

D ☐ Increase by 10%

Forecasting cash flows 1

CASH FLOW is the money flowing into and out of a business on a day-to-day basis. A CASH-FLOW FORECAST predicts how cash will flow through a business over time. A business can use it to identify periods where it could have a CASH-FLOW PROBLEM, where it does not have enough money flowing into the business to pay its day-to-day bills.

Cash-flow forecasts

Inflows / receipts – e.g. money from owners, bank loans or cash from sales.

Outflows / payments – e.g. wages, raw materials, interest on loans, advertising or bills.

Net cash flow – the receipts of a business minus its payments, either positive or negative.

Opening balance – the amount of money in a business at the start of a month.

	SEPT	OCT	NOV	DEC
Total receipts	8000	8500	13 500	15 000
Payments				
Machinery and equipment	10 000	0	0	0
Wages and materials	4400	4400	6000	4000
Heating, lighting and insurance	0	3500	1000	0
Total payments	14 400	7900	7000	4000
Net cash flow	–6400	600	6500	11 000
Opening balance	0	–6400	–5800	700
Closing balance	–6400	–5800	700	11 700

Cumulative cash flow – the sum of cash that flows into a business over time.

Closing balance – the amount of money in a business at the end of a month (net cash flow + opening balance).

Worked example

target B-A

Fill in the **four** blanks to complete this table. **(4 marks)**

	Jan	Feb	Mar
Receipts (£)	10 000	8500	15 000
Payments (£)			
Raw materials	2000	2500	3600
Fixed costs	4000	4000	4000
Other costs	5000	5200	5900
Total payments	**11 000**	**11 700**	**13 500**
Net cash flow	–1000	–3200	1500
Opening balance	500	–500	–3700
Closing balance	–500	–3700	–2200

An exam question could ask you to fill in the blanks on a cash-flow forecast. Use the following to help you.

- RECEIPTS. Add net cash flow and total payments.
- PAYMENTS. A missing payment can be found by adding up the rest and taking it away from total payments.
- TOTAL PAYMENTS. Add up all payments or subtract net cash flow from receipts.
- NET CASH FLOW. Subtract total payments from receipts or deduct the closing balance from the opening balance.
- OPENING BALANCE. This is always the previous month's closing balance.
- CLOSING BALANCE. Add the net cash flow to the opening balance.

Now try this

target B-A

A business has the following cash-flow information for one particular month.
Opening balance: £5000   Cash inflow: £7000   Cash outflow: £14 000

1   What is the closing balance for the business at the end of the month? Select **one** answer. **(1 mark)**

 A ☐ –£12 000   B ☐ –£2000   C ☐ £9000   D ☐ £16 000

Forecasting cash flows 2

It is important for a business to understand the factors that affect its cash flow and also how cash-flow problems can lead to insolvency.

Change in sales revenue / change in demand

Change in costs (commodity prices)

Credit terms can change (period of time or amount needed to pay a bill or invoice)

What impacts on cash flow?

Seasonality in sales (such as sun cream)

Change in stock levels

Business expansion or contraction

Cash flow and insolvency

Without sufficient cash within the business a business would become INSOLVENT. This means that it would be unable to:

- pay its debts
- repay bank loans
- pay wages to employees
- buy raw materials and products to sell
- promote the business.

Cash flow, profit and risk

Cash flow is not profit. A profitable business may still have a cash-flow problem and go out of business.

Cash flow is an important part of any BUSINESS PLAN. Planning to avoid cash-flow problems can reduce RISK.

Worked example

target C–B

Which **two** of the following are the most likely ways that PrintZone Ltd could improve its cash flow position? Select **two** answers.   (2 marks)

A ☐ Use a mind map to improve financial planning

B ☐ Carry out quantitative market research

C ☒ Increase revenue by improving sales

D ☒ Negotiate lower prices with suppliers

E ☐ Employ two more full-time members of staff

EXAM ALERT!

Just under half of students scored both marks for this question. The question asks which methods are **most likely** to improve its cash flow position. Market research might help in the longer term but Options C and D are more immediate and obvious ways to improve cash flow.

This was a real exam question that a lot of students struggled with – **be prepared!**   ResultsPlus

Now try this

target C–B

1 Monthly sales at PrintZone remain unchanged from April to October. Given this fact, which **two** of the following are possible reasons for the worsening cash-flow position of the business during this time? Select **two** answers.   (2 marks)

A ☐ Increased spending on stocks of ink cartridges and printers by PrintZone

B ☐ Change in the interest rate on PrintZone's bank loan from 5% to 4%

C ☐ Monthly rent on PrintZone's premises changing from £700 to £650

D ☐ More favourable trade credit terms provided by suppliers to PrintZone

E ☐ PrintZone's monthly advertising costs changing from £800 to £1400

The business plan

A BUSINESS PLAN is a plan for the development of a business, giving forecasts of items such as sales, costs and cash flow.

The purpose of a business plan

A business owner may write a business plan to:

- convince a bank to loan the business money
- forecast financial projections
- identify the needs of customers
- formulate market research into important information, e.g. about competitors
- provide information, e.g. about competitors
- provide the owner with a 'plan of action' that will minimise risk.

The business plan links together other sections of your course. For example, a business plan will include a cash-flow forecast and business objectives, and it will help an entrepreneur to answer important questions about their business, such as 'What if?' questions. As a result, a business plan can help reduce the risk of starting a business.

What goes into a business plan?

Overview
Name, location, type of business and its purpose (i.e. the products it will sell).

Objectives
What the business hopes to achieve in a specific period of time (e.g. in the first six months or within three years).

Market Research
Size, growth, features and trends in the market.

Personnel
Who will work within the business and what their roles will be.

Finances
Sources of finance, cash-flow forecasts, revenues, cost and profits.

Production
Information on suppliers and how products will be made and supplied.

Worked example

target D-C

Which **three** of the following would Marie have had to include in her business plan?
Select **three** answers. **(3 marks)**

A ☐ All her invoices and receipts from purchases and sales

B ☐ A copy of the design of her business card

C ☒ A cash-flow forecast

D ☐ A record of all her profits from the business for the past five years

E ☒ An overview of the nature of the business

F ☒ A summary of the market research she has carried out

In this answer, Options A and D are not feasible, as Marie would not have this information before she started her business. Neither are these financial records necessary in a business plan. Option B is irrelevant, as a design of a business card would provide little useful information. Options C, E and F are all relevant information normally included in a business plan.

Now try this

target C-B

1   Which **two** of the following are the most likely reasons to produce a business plan?
Select **two** answers. **(2 marks)**

A ☐ To show off the skills of the entrepreneur

B ☐ To get support from a bank

C ☐ To show other people you can create a business plan

D ☐ To convince customers to buy from the business

E ☐ To help monitor actual sales against forecast sales

Obtaining finance 1

Long-term sources of finance

- Share capital (for limited companies only, not sole traders).
- Personal savings (from the owner).
- Venture capitalist (external investor looking for fast growth and return on their investment).
- Grants.

- Loans (from a lender such as a bank).
- Mortgage (a loan secured against a property).
- Retained profit (if there is any).
- Leasing (renting a property, equipment or vehicle instead of buying it).

Selling shares

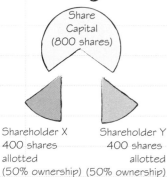

Share Capital (800 shares)

Shareholder X
400 shares allotted
(50% ownership)

Shareholder Y
400 shares allotted
(50% ownership)

A share is a part-ownership in a business. A start-up, that is a limited company, can sell SHARES to potential investors to raise capital. These investors are then SHAREHOLDERS in the business and are entitled to a share of any profits generated.

Security (Collateral)

Often when money is borrowed the lender will be given some form of security or COLLATERAL against the loan. In the case of a mortgage this is the property. The incentive for a bank to loan money is the INTEREST they will receive. The rate of interest or nature of the security determines the level of risk associated with lending the money. That's why an entrepreneur is a risk taker!

Worked example

target C-B

As a sole trader, which **three** of the following are long-term sources of finance for Sonia? Select **three** answers.   **(3 marks)**

A ☒ Profit   D ☐ Trade credit

B ☐ Overdraft   E ☐ Share capital

C ☒ Bank loan   F ☒ Personal savings

Options B and D are **short-term sources** of finance (short-term sources are covered on page 24), leaving Options A, C and F as correct long-term sources.

EXAM ALERT!

Only two in ten students got all three marks for this question. The context of this question is a 'sole trader' and not a limited company. Only limited companies can raise capital through selling shares.

This was a real exam question that a lot of students struggled with – **be prepared!**   Results **Plus**

Now try this

target C-B

Mark is a qualified hairdresser looking to set up as a sole trader. Mark is considering different sources of finance to start his business.

1   Which **two** of the following would be **most appropriate** for Mark to start up his business? Select **two** answers.   **(2 marks)**

A ☐ Personal savings   D ☐ Retained profit

B ☐ Selling the business's assets   E ☐ Bank loan

C ☐ Issuing shares to new shareholders

Obtaining finance 2

Businesses may require finance in the short term, as well as from long-term sources (see page 23 for more on long-term finance). Short-term sources of finance are sources that are repaid immediately or fairly quickly, usually within a year.

Bank overdraft

Delayed payment (some businesses may try to delay payments to reduce cash outflows)

Short-term sources of finance

Trade credit

Credit cards (short-term borrowing)

Factoring (receiving cash immediately from a factor, such as a bank, instead of waiting to be paid)

You should know the causes of cash-flow problems and have some ideas about how a business could improve its cash flow. Short-term sources such as trade credit and overdrafts are suitable solutions to help solve cash-flow problems.

Worked example

 target C-B

What would be the most appropriate way that Sparkle Oven Cleaning Company Ltd could cope with its negative cash flow in August and September? Select **one** answer.   **(1 mark)**

A ☐ Approach its bank to take out a loan

B ☐ Sell more shares in the company

C ☒ Arrange an overdraft with its bank

D ☐ Seek out the services of a venture capitalist

 Cash flow is an immediate issue and therefore it requires a short-term source of finance to resolve the problem. Option C is an 'overdraft' and the only short-term source of finance mentioned.

Now try this

target C-B

1 Match the terms on the left with the correct definitions on the right.   **(4 marks)**

	Term		Definition
Grants	i	a	Receiving cash immediately from a third party, instead of waiting to be paid. Debt is then passed on to the third party to collect.
Venture capitalist	ii	b	An individual or company that buys shares in what they hope will be a fast-growing company.
Overdraft	iii	c	An amount of money provided to a business from the government or a charity, which does not have to be repaid.
Factoring	iv	d	A short-term loan allowing a business to overspend on their bank account up to a limit and with interest charged.
		e	A source of finance where owners are entitled to a share of any profits generated.

Customer focus

Understanding customers and focusing on their needs is a vital if a business intends to attract people to buy their products. There are three stages of being CUSTOMER FOCUSED.

Being customer focused

1 Identifying needs – using techniques such as market research to find out what customers want.

2 Anticipating needs – the best businesses are able to identify needs in advance to give them a competitive advantage.

3 Meeting customer needs – a business must be able to provide whatever customers want, whether that is quality, low prices or excellent service.

Customer focus in practice

A business asking customers to complete a questionnaire as they leave the store.

A pub opening a beer garden, anticipating warm weather, or a fashion brand changing clothing in its stores to match the styles at a national fashion show.

A business adapting elements of the marketing mix, e.g. using recycled packaging for environmentally conscious customers.

Worked example

target D-C

Sparkle Oven Cleaning Company Ltd offers an oven cleaning service. The owner, Eddie Lowe, says the focus of the business is competitive prices, high standards and good customer service.

Which **one** of the following might be a key part of the customer focus for Sparkle Oven Cleaning Company Ltd? Select **one** answer.   **(1 mark)**

A ☒ Making sure that appointments are kept on time

B ☐ Ensuring staff do the job in as short a time as possible to maximise sales

C ☐ Monitoring competitors and charging slightly higher prices than them

D ☐ Managing a business so it can make the maximum profit possible

Customer focus is about identifying, anticipating and meeting customer needs. Option A is the only answer that is focused on the customer and not either driven by profit maximisation or in the interests of the business itself.

Now try this

target F-E

1 Which **two** of the following would be essential elements of customer focus for a business?   **(2 marks)**

A ☐ Anticipating customer needs

B ☐ Ordering stocks of raw materials

C ☐ Providing customers with what they want

D ☐ Paying customer tax

E ☐ Paying employees

The marketing mix

1 **Product**

The PRODUCT itself has to meet the needs of customers and have the correct attributes and features that the customer wants. A successful business will try to differentiate their products.

2 **Place**

PLACE is the way in which a product is distributed – how it gets from the producer to the consumer. Businesses have to consider the channel (e.g. online or through retail stores). For example, a luxury suit might be sold in an upmarket boutique on Bond Street in London.

3 **Promotion**

PROMOTION is communication between the business and customer that makes the customer aware of its products, including:
- advertising
- sales promotions
- sponsorship
- public relations.

4 **Price**

The PRICE of a product must reflect the value customers place on the product. High-quality products have a high price. Customers are also willing to pay more for special features. Price is very subjective because it depends on many factors, such as commodity prices (see page 31) and the price set by competitors.

Worked example

target
C-B

Lisa believes there is a market for gardening services and has carried out market research. Some of her results are shown below.

What is the most important factor in the decision to choose a gardening service?	
	Number of responses as a percentage
Price of the service	12
Quality of the work	41
Advertisement in the local paper	16
Customer service	20

According to the table, which element of the marketing mix should Lisa focus on in her business?
Select **one** answer.   **(1 mark)**

A ☐ Place   C ☒ Product

B ☐ Price   D ☐ Promotion

From the table we can see that 'quality of the work' and 'customer service' receive the highest responses. These two factors contribute to the 'product' that Lisa provides in her gardening business.

Now try this

target
B-A

Chocolicious is a small business making handmade chocolates. The market it operates in is very competitive. One source of competitive advantage it holds is in the quality of its chocolates. The owners are worried by the recent rise in the price of cocoa.

1 Chocolicious has decided that it needs to change its marketing mix in response to the rising price of cocoa. Which **two** changes to the marketing mix would you advise, given what is happening in this market? Select **two** answers.   **(2 marks)**

A ☐ Reducing its Corporation Tax payments

B ☐ Producing a new business plan

C ☐ Contacting supermarkets to seek new retailers for its products

D ☐ Making five members of staff redundant to cut costs

E ☐ Using cheaper ingredients in the product

Limited liability

The term LIABILITY refers to the legal responsibility of a business towards its debts.

Unlimited liability

Owner and business are the same

Sole traders (or sole proprietors) are businesses owned by one person. The owner has UNLIMITED LIABILITY. The owner is legally responsible for any debts of the business. Therefore there is potential for the owner to lose his or her personal belongings to pay off any debts.

Limited liability

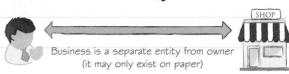

Business is a separate entity from owner (it may only exist on paper)

Private limited companies (Ltd) have LIMITED LIABILITY. The owners and the business are separate legal entities. Any debts incurred by the business belong to the business and the owners can only lose up to the amount that they have invested. Their personal belongings are not liable.

The differences between sole traders and Ltds

	Sole traders	Private limited companies
Risk	Unlimited liability means there is more risk.	Limited liability reduces the risk for the owners.
Control	The owner has 100% control of decisions.	The control of the main owner will depend on the proportion of the business sold as shares to other shareholders.
Profits	The owners keep 100% of the profits.	Profits are shared proportionately between the shares owned by shareholders.
Privacy	There is more privacy.	Accounts are filed with Companies House and can be viewed by anyone on payment of a small fee.

Worked example

target C-B

Which **two** of the following might be the most likely reasons why someone might set up as a private limited company? Select **two** answers.   **(2 marks)**

A ☐ She wants to raise lots of money on the Stock Exchange

B ☒ She believes the risk would be less

C ☐ She wants to be the sole owner of the business

D ☐ She would have access to limited sources of finance

E ☒ She would be liable only for the amount she invested if the business failed

Option A is incorrect, as a private limited company is not allowed to sell its shares through the Stock Market. Options C and D do not apply to a private limited company.

Now try this

target F-E

1   Identify **one** disadvantage of unlimited liability for a sole trader. Select **one** answer.   **(1 mark)**

A ☐ The need to pay higher taxes

B ☐ Less control of the business

C ☐ Sharing profit with other shareholders

D ☐ Risk of losing personal possessions

Start-up legal and tax issues

There are regulations and tax issues that all businesses have to adhere to. Every business must keep up-to-date records on its business activity, and trade under a unique name.

Why have legislation?

Businesses have to adhere to legal requirements:

- so that the government can keep a track of business activity
- so taxes can be collected
- to protect businesses from illegal activity
- to protect customers from illegal business practices.

The legal requirements of a small business

- Register and trade under a unique name that promotes the business (a limited company will have Ltd at the end).
- Keep records of sales, purchases and names of businesses they have worked with.
- Register with Her Majesty's Revenue & Customs (HMRC – the government authority in the UK responsible for collecting tax).
- Pay the appropriate level of tax to HMRC.

Value Added Tax (VAT) – a tax on the value of sales of a business. Businesses that sell more than a certain amount will register to pay VAT.

Taxes on small businesses

Income tax – a tax on the income earned by workers and sole traders.

National Insurance Contributions (NIC) – a tax on earnings of workers and sole traders linked to state benefits.

Corporation tax – a tax paid by limited companies on the profits of the company.

Worked example

target
D-C

Marcus Borega is a sole trader. His business imports high-quality cars from the USA.

Which **two** of the following taxes will Marcus have to pay in the course of running his business? Select **two** answers.   **(2 marks)**

A ☐ Corporation tax   D ☐ Labour tax

B ☐ Distribution tax   E ☒ National Insurance Contributions

C ☒ Income tax

EXAM ALERT!

Only one in five students scored both marks for this question. Know your taxes and which types of businesses have to pay them. As Marcus is a sole trader he is required to pay Income Tax and National Insurance Contributions. Remember, National Insurance Contributions are still a tax even though 'tax' does not appear in the name.

This was a real exam question that a lot of students struggled with – **be prepared!**   ResultsPlus

---

Now try this

target
D-C

Marie set up a new private limited company selling gift bags.

1 Which **one** of the following would be the **most likely** reasons why Marie has to keep a record of her business's income and spending? Select **one** answer.   **(1 mark)**

A ☐ So that she could return any faulty goods she bought to the shop

B ☐ To be able to prove to Her Majesty's Revenue & Customs that she is paying the right amount of tax

C ☐ To be able to prove to her family that she is running the business properly

D ☐ So that if she made a loss she could see what item of spending caused the loss

Customer satisfaction

CUSTOMER SATISFACTION is a measure of how much a business or its products meet customers' expectations.

Good customer service

To meet the needs of customers, businesses must provide effective CUSTOMER SERVICE. How can they do this?

- Dispatching orders quickly.
- Being 100% accurate in orders / deliveries.
- Offering excellent after-sales care.
- Providing a personal service.
- Going the 'extra mile' to get what customers want.
- Being convenient.
- Being polite and friendly.
- Responding immediately to any complaints.

Providing a personal service is an example of good customer service.

Benefits of good customer satisfaction

- ☑ Repeat purchase.
- ☑ Loyalty.
- ☑ Business can charge a premium price.
- ☑ Improves business reputation (good public relations and word of mouth).
- ☑ Can differentiate a business and become their USP.

Keeping the customer coming back

REPEAT PURCHASES help achieve long-term sales and therefore the success of a business. Repeat purchases can be stimulated through:

- cheaper prices than competitors
- easy and convenient service
- effective customer service
- promotions and special offers
- building good relationships with customers (good communication).

Worked example

target E-D

Martin Hudson runs Buckingham Ltd, a business selling high-quality office furniture to other businesses.

In this question, only Options B and D have anything to do with improving the service to customers. Option A might be a benefit from high levels of customer satisfaction, but it will not achieve it.

Which **two** of the following are likely to be the most effective methods that Buckingham might use to deliver high levels of customer satisfaction?
Select **two** answers.　　　　　　**(2 marks)**

A ☐ Securing repeat purchases by customers

B ☒ Fulfilling customer orders accurately

C ☐ Setting non-financial objectives

D ☒ Introducing a 24-hour customer helpline

E ☐ Advertising on local radio stations

Now try this

target F-E

1　Which of the following is a reason why customer service is important to the success of a small business?
Select **one** answer.　　　　　　**(1 mark)**

A ☐ Customers are the ones who add value

B ☐ A small business wants to get repeat purchases

C ☐ Customers will buy a product if the price is right

D ☐ It has to meet legal requirements

Recruiting, training and motivating

As small businesses grow they may employ workers to fill new roles in the business. Businesses want the RIGHT EMPLOYEES FOR THE JOB. The recruitment process is crucial in achieving this.

The recruitment process

Draw up recruitment documents
Including job adverts, job particulars, job descriptions and job specifications

Receive applications
Through CVs, application forms and letters

Shortlisting
A list of suitable candidates is drawn up

Selection
Involves interviews and assessments; references might be requested

Training
To develop skills using on-the-job and off-the-job training (all staff, but especially new staff)

The candidate selected must have the right SKILLS (e.g. the ability to operate computers or machines) and ATTITUDES (e.g. flexibility or hardworking).

Motivation

A motivated workforce will be more committed and productive. A business can motivate staff by:

- paying fair and competitive wages
- providing good working conditions
- providing perks, such as company cars
- delegating power and responsibility
- training and nurturing staff development
- encouraging teamwork and good relationships.

Employment legislation

Employers must abide by laws that protect employees in a number of areas:

- Recruitment – employees cannot discriminate on the basis of sex, age, gender or disability.
- Pay – employees must be paid equally for doing the same job.
- Discipline – employees are protected from unfair dismissal.
- Working hours – employees cannot be expected to work over a certain number of hours.

Worked example

target B-A

Which **three** of the following documents are used in the recruitment process? Select **three** answers.   **(3 marks)**

A ☒ Job description
B ☐ Business plan
C ☐ Person description
D ☒ Job advert
E ☒ Application form
F ☐ Cash flow forecast

Now try this

target D-C

1 Which **one** of the following might be the most effective method of motivation for workers? Select **one** answer.

A ☐ They are given free pens
B ☐ They are given a book on motivational theories
C ☐ The quality and range of training they are given gives them confidence to perform their role well
D ☐ They are paid a bonus

Market demand and supply

The prices of GOODS and COMMODITIES change constantly. These changes in price are influenced by the relationship between SUPPLY and DEMAND.

Supply for a product is the amount that sellers are willing and able to sell at any given price.

SUPPLY ⟹

Farmers supply wheat to make flour

Demand for a product is the amount that buyers are willing and able to purchase at any given price.

DEMAND ⟹

Bakers demand flour to make bread

The surplus and shortage of commodities in a market will affect prices. ⟹

Demand	Supply	Impact
High	Low	SHORTAGE – prices rise
Low	High	SURPLUS – prices fall

Market differences

- A MARKET is where buyers and sellers meet to exchange products and services.
- COMMODITY MARKETS are markets for raw materials, such as oil, steel and wheat, used in the production of other goods.
- GOODS MARKETS (normal markets) are markets for everyday products, such as clothes and food.

Costs

Changes in raw material and energy costs affect the costs of small businesses. How much it affects them will depend on:

- their proportion of total costs (a great deal, greatly affected)
- how much costs go up (a little, not greatly affected)
- the ability to pass on costs to customers or to absorb them (passed on, not greatly affected).

Worked example

target **A–A***

Which **three** factors below are the most likely causes of the rise in price of cocoa? Select **three** answers.   **(3 marks)**

- A ☐ Lower demand for cocoa from chocolate producers
- B ☐ Increased profits made by cocoa producers
- C ☒ News reports suggesting some health benefits from cocoa
- D ☐ Greater supply of cocoa by producers
- E ☒ Poor weather leading to a poor harvest of cocoa
- F ☒ Higher demand for cocoa by chocolate manufacturers

EXAM ALERT!

Three in ten students got all three marks for this question. A rise in the price of cocoa would be caused by a fall in supply and / or an increase in demand.

This was a real exam question that a lot of students struggled with – **be prepared!**

Now try this

target **B–A**

Pasta is made from wheat. In 2009, good weather led to a large increase in the wheat harvest.

1 Which of the following is the most likely effect of this increase?
Select **one** answer.   **(1 mark)**

- A ☐ The price of wheat will fall
- C ☐ The cost of wheat will rise
- B ☐ People will have to pay more for their pasta
- D ☐ The demand for wheat will fall

The impact of interest rates

An INTEREST RATE is the percentage reward or payment over a period of time that is given to savers on savings or paid by borrowers on loans.

The cost of borrowing

An entrepreneur or small business may not have capital to start or expand a business without borrowing. Typically a bank will give a LOAN to a business or allow it to have an OVERDRAFT. The business will pay INTEREST:

- on top of its repayments for the loan
- on any amount it is overdrawn.

This is the cost of borrowing money and the incentive for a bank to lend it.

Fixed and variable interest rates

Fixed interest rates do not change over the life of a loan. A business could lose out on a fixed contract if the rate falls.

Variable interest rates change over the life of a loan. They can be more risky and hard for a business to plan against.

A RISE in interest rates will INCREASE the cost of borrowing.

- Businesses on a variable rate may struggle to repay loans.
- Small businesses are less likely to borrow money to start up or to expand.
- Customers are less likely to spend money as borrowed money costs more, so consumer spending falls.

A FALL in interest rates will LOWER the cost of borrowing.

- Businesses will have more money to spend and cash flow may improve.
- Businesses may borrow money for a start-up or expansion.
- Customers are more likely to borrow and to spend their money. Consumer spending rises.

Worked example

target D-C

During Sonia's first year of trading, interest rates increased from 3% to 5%. Identify **three** possible effects of this on her business.

Select **three** answers. **(3 marks)**

A ☐ A reduction in fixed costs due to lower repayments on her overdraft

B ☒ A worsening net cash-flow position

C ☐ A rise in sales due to higher levels of consumer spending

D ☐ A greater chance of rivals entering the market

E ☒ A fall in sales due to lower levels of consumer spending

F ☒ An increase in fixed costs due to higher repayments on her overdraft

An increase in interest rates is generally a bad thing for small businesses.

Now try this

target D-C

1 If interest rates rose in the UK, which **two** of the following would be the most likely effects on a small business? Select **two** answers. **(2 marks)**

The business would:

A ☐ see no difference because it did not have any savings

B ☐ see its costs rise

C ☐ see its costs falling

D ☐ see its sales slow down

E ☐ see its sales rise because customers are now more interested

Changes in exchange rates

The EXCHANGE RATE is the price of buying foreign currency. It tells UK people and businesses how much foreign currency they get for every pound, or how many pounds they have to give up to acquire foreign currency.

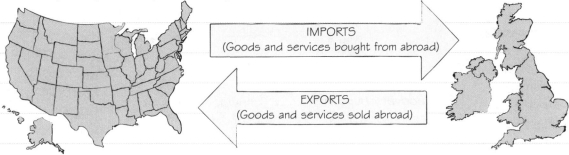

IMPORTS
(Goods and services bought from abroad)

EXPORTS
(Goods and services sold abroad)

Calculating the cost of foreign exchange

Exports: £1 = $2

- £500 of goods sold to a business in the USA cost $1000 (500 × 2)

Imports: £1 = $2

- $600 of goods bought by a UK business cost £300 (600 ÷ 2)

The effect of a fall in the value of the pound	The effect of a rise in the value of the pound
Good for UK exporters of goods – price of exports falls ➡ sales increase.	Bad for UK exporters of goods – price of exports rises ➡ sales fall.
Good for UK tourism – prices cheaper to foreigners ➡ tourism increases.	Bad for UK tourism – prices more expensive to foreigners ➡ tourism falls.
Good for UK businesses – imports more expensive ➡ people buy more UK goods.	Bad for UK businesses – imports cheaper ➡ people buy fewer UK goods.
Bad for UK importers of materials – imports more expensive ➡ costs rise.	Good for UK importers of materials – imports cheaper ➡ costs fall.

Worked example

target
B-A

A business has the following costs in June.

	June
Raw materials imported from USA	£10 000
Raw materials from UK	£7000
Fixed costs	£11 000
Exchange rate	£1 = $1.50

In June £10 000 raw materials actually costs $15 000 (10 000 × 1.5). In July the business still requires $15 000 worth of raw materials, but as the pound is now stronger it will cost only £9375 ($15 000 ÷ 1.6). Costs have therefore fallen by £625 (£10 000 – £9375). Assuming everything else remains the same, this will increase profit by £625.

In June the business makes £11 000 profit. In July, the exchange rate has changed to £1 = $1.60.

Assuming all other data remain the same, what effect does this change have on the profit level? Select **one** answer. **(1 mark)**

A ☐ Decrease by £1350   B ☐ Remain the same   C ☒ Increase by £625   D ☐ Increase by £1600

Now try this

target
B-A

1   Charles buys 100 kg of pasta a month. The price of pasta is €5 per kg. In April, the exchange rate is £1 = €1.25. How much will this cost Charles in pounds sterling? Select **one** answer. **(1 mark)**

A ☐ £625   B ☐ £500   C ☐ £400   D ☐ £250

The business cycle

The business cycle refers to fluctuations in the level of economic activity over time. Businesses are affected by the business cycle in different ways. A business selling essentials, such as food, will not be as affected as a business selling luxuries, such as new cars or cruise holidays.

Economic activity refers to the amount of buying and selling that takes place between businesses and consumers in a period of time. If this rises it is known as **economic growth**.

Boom
Strong increase in economic activity.

Recovery / upturn
Economic activity begins to rise.

Slowdown / downturn
Economic activity begins to slow down.

Recession
When economic growth is negative (less than the period before).

The government may take action in a boom, e.g. raising interest rates to control spending and price rises.

In a downturn it may cut interest rates to reduce costs and encourage spending.

In a boom

- Consumer and business confidence high.
- Consumers borrow and spend more.
- Sales increase.
- Businesses take on more employees.
- Businesses invest and expand.

In a downturn or recession

- Consumer and business confidence low.
- Consumers borrow and spend less, preferring to save.
- Sales fall. Prices may have to be cut.
- Businesses may make some employees redundant.
- Businesses save and cut back on spending.
- Businesses more likely to experience cash-flow problems.

Worked example

 target C-B

Identify **three** likely effects on a small business of a downturn in the business cycle. Select **three** answers. **(3 marks)**

A ☐ Higher sales owing to rising consumer incomes

B ☒ Lower fixed costs owing to lower interest rates

C ☐ Less risk of the business becoming insolvent

D ☐ More difficulty recruiting employees

E ☒ Lower demand owing to business closures

F ☒ Lower prices on goods bought from suppliers

In a downturn there is likely to be a fall in spending. This may result in closures and falls in prices. The government may act in a downturn by lowering interest rates.

Now try this

target C-B

Pink Ladies is a taxi service for women only, based in Warrington.

1 Which **two** of the following might lead to a fall in sales for the Pink Ladies taxi service? Select **two** answers. **(2 marks)**

A ☐ A rise in unemployment in Warrington

B ☐ A rise in the prices charged by other taxi firms in Warrington

C ☐ A fall in interest rates

D ☐ A reduction in the price of late night bus fares in Warrington

E ☐ An upturn in the business cycle

34

Business decisions and stakeholders

A STAKEHOLDER is an individual or a group that has an interest in and is affected by the activities of a business.

Managers – want bonuses and long-term success

Owners (shareholders) – want profits and a return on their investment

Workers – want good pay and working conditions

Suppliers – want regular orders

Stakeholders

Customers – want value for money

Government – wants low unemployment and competitive markets

The local community – wants local investment and limited pollution

Competitors – sometimes want cooperation and support

A business has an impact upon and can be affected by their stakeholders. Therefore, business decisions must take into account stakeholder needs.

Stakeholders may have conflicting interests. It can be difficult for a business to meet everyone's needs.

Stakeholder conflicts

Local community complains about traffic congestion

Bad publicity leads to falling sales

As a result, the company halves its usual order value from suppliers

Customers are unhappy with prices and sales fall further

Company guarantees employees bonuses in the following year by raising prices

In order to maintain profits for owners, employee bonuses are withheld

Employees are unhappy with fall in incomes

Worked example

target **F-E**

The Elm Tree is a successful traditional pub in the village of Elmton and is owned by Jeremy Cousins. He has decided to use land behind the pub to build a private function room for weddings and events.

Which stakeholder is the extension most likely to have a negative impact on? Select **one** answer. **(1 mark)**

A ☐ Customers B ☐ Government C ☒ Local residents D ☐ Employees

Each stakeholder is relevant to Jeremy's business. The correct answer is Option C because the local residents may be concerned that building work in their village could cause noise and disruption.

Now try this

target **G-F**

Cantwell's is a business that makes zips for clothing. It decides to make five workers redundant.

1 Which **one** of the following stakeholders is most likely to benefit from this decision. Select **one** answer. **(1 mark)**

A ☐ Suppliers and the business because they will now sell more zips to Cantwell's

B ☐ The local community because there will now be more spending in local shops

C ☐ The government because it will now collect more in tax

D ☐ The owners because their costs will fall

Exam skills 1

You will have 45 minutes to complete the Unit 1 exam paper. The paper is worth 40 marks and will contain multiple choice and objective test questions. These questions test your knowledge and understanding of a topic. They usually test your knowledge of key terms so make sure you have revised these.

Multiple choice questions

When tackling multiple choice questions:

- ✓ underline the key terms in the question
- ✓ read all the options carefully
- ✓ rule out the ones you know are wrong
- ✓ select what you think is the right answer
- ✓ double check the remaining options.

Choosing the best answers

You need to be really careful when you are choosing your answers. There are often choices which look sensible, but aren't suitable for the CONTEXT of the question. Always read the question carefully and choose the MOST APPROPRIATE options for the context.

Worked example

target G-F

Which **two** of the following are **most important** in spotting a new business opportunity?
Select **two** answers.   **(2 marks)**

A ☒ Recognising a need in the market place
B ☐ Being able to sell at a low price
C ☐ Knowing someone who has already started a business
D ☒ Knowing who your competitors are
E ☐ Being a brilliant accountant

This question is asking you to find the two **most important** options.

Options C and E are not relevant to spotting a business opportunity so are not good choices.

Option B is a possibility because a new business might be more competitive by selling at a low price. However, this is not the **most important** thing when spotting a new business opportunity.

Options A and D are the correct answers.

Worked example

target E-D

JayCD is a small independent CD music store which operates on very narrow profit margins. It is facing strong competition from a local supermarket in the town selling chart CDs at very low prices.

Which **two** of the following are the **most likely** methods JayCD might use to compete with the local supermarket?   **(2 marks)**
Select **two** answers.

A ☐ Lower its prices below the supermarket
B ☐ Launch an advertising campaign on national television
C ☒ Provide an ordering service for hard-to-find CDs for their customers
D ☐ Open up two new stores in the town
E ☒ Improve the quality of customer service

Some multiple choice questions will have a case study. You will need to think carefully about the context when you are answering the question.

Start by underlining the key points in the case study. Then look at each of the options in the context of these key points.

Option A is not a likely method as the company already has a very narrow profit margin.

Options B and D are likely to be too expensive for a small, independent company.

Options C and E will allow JayCD to create competitive advantages by offering a specialist service and quality customer service.

Exam skills 2

Some questions in the Unit 1 exam require you to calculate the correct answer from a set of figures, so make sure you revise your formulae as well as key terms for the exam.

Calculations

- ✓ Read all the information carefully.
- ✓ Make sure you understand what the figures in the question are showing you.
- ✓ Identify the formula you need to use.
- ✓ Work out the correct answer – write your workings on the exam paper if you need to.
- ✓ Double-check the remaining option/s.

Matching definitions

You might be asked to match key terms to the correct definitions in the exam.

When answering these questions, take time to read through all the definitions and key terms first before matching any. Some might be quite similar, so make sure you take the appropriate time to choose the correct answers.

 Make sure it's clear which key term you are linking to which definition.

Worked example

 target B–A

The following table shows the costs, revenues and profits for a business for the first three months of the year.

Fill in the **five blanks** to complete the table.

	January	February	March	
Total receipts	£24 000	£30 000	£32 000	i
Fixed costs	£3000	£3000	£3000	ii
Variable costs	£6000	£7500	£8000	iii
Total costs	£9000	£10 500	£11 000	iv
Profit	£15 000	£19 500	£21 000	v

(5 marks)

i   Total receipts = total costs + profit
   = £10 500 + £19 500 = **£30 000**

ii   Fixed costs = **£3000**

iii   Variable costs = total costs – fixed costs
   = £11 000 – £3000 = **£8000**

iv   Total costs = total receipts – profit
   = £32 000 – £21 000 = **£11 000**

v   Profit = total receipts – total costs
   = £24 000 – £9000 = **£15 000**

Now try this

 target A–A*

1   Match the definition on the left with the correct term on the right. Select the definition and then the term. There is only **one** correct term for each definition.

	Definition		Term
Information about opinions, judgements and attitudes	i	a	Quantitative data
Goods or services sold to foreign buyers	ii	b	Imports
Part of a market that contains a group of buyers with similar buying habits	iii	c	Market map
Raw materials such as coal, oil, copper, iron ore and wheat	iv	d	Exports
The way in which a business sets out the key features of its market	v	e	Qualitative data
		f	Market segment
		g	Commodities
		h	Marketing mix

EXAM ALERT!

One in three students got full marks for this question. Make sure that you read the terms and definitions carefully.

This was a real exam question that a lot of students struggled with – **be prepared!** ResultsPlus

Exam skills 3

If you are taking the GCSE Business Studies Short Course, you will take the Unit 6 exam. You will have 45 minutes to complete the Unit 6 exam paper. The paper is worth 40 marks and will contain multiple-choice, objective-test and extended-answer questions.

Extended-answer question

The extended-answer question in the Unit 6 exam paper is worth six marks. You will be given a business scenario and will be asked to make a choice between two options. To answer these questions effectively you should:

☑ Read the question carefully.

☑ Choose one of the options.

☑ Make clearly developed points to justify your choice.

☑ Support your points with appropriate examples.

☑ Ensure that your written work is a high standard, with an appropriate structure and few, or no, errors in spelling, punctuation and grammar.

Worked example

Martin O'Brien owns a successful sandwich bar in a busy town centre. He employs three part-time staff and has built up a good reputation over recent years. He is now finding that competition is increasing. Other firms that provide sandwiches such as Subway, Greggs and Pret A Manger, as well as supermarkets, are his main competitors.

Martin has decided that he needs to add more value to his product to compete.

Which of the following methods of adding value would you choose if you were Martin? Justify your choice.

Option chosen (tick **one** box only)

☐ **Choice 1:** Convenience – improving the time in which customers are served. This will require him to take on an extra worker.

☑ **Choice 2:** Quality – increasing the quality of ingredients.   **(6 marks)**

Increasing the quality of ingredients could add value by creating a unique selling point for Martin's sandwiches. This will help the shop to stand out against the competition. However, the competitors are all big brands such as Subway and Greggs which already have a reputation for quality products so...

This is an extract from a student answer.

There is no right or wrong answer and you could choose **convenience** or **quality** to add value. Whichever one you choose you must support your decision with appropriate business understanding.

EXAM ALERT!

One in four students scored five or six marks for this question. This question asks about **adding value** so you need to refer specifically to this in your answer. Many students wrote about what the business should do to improve generally, and did not consider how the business could add value.

This was a real exam question that a lot of students struggled with – **be prepared!**

Marketing

Marketing involves identifying and understanding customer needs and wants. Businesses can then provide products and services that meet these needs PROFITABLY. Remember that marketing is about UNDERSTANDING customers, not just selling.

The marketing process

Market research to identify and understand customers

Developing and testing products and services

Communicating products and services to customers

Why bother?

Businesses need to think about marketing in order to:

☑ reduce risk of product failure

☑ understand their customers

☑ communicate products effectively to encourage customers to buy them

☑ keep up to date with market trends so products can continue to meet customer needs.

Market segmentation

A market segment is a group of customers in a market that have similar characteristics and needs. You can segment the car market by the type of car a person drives, such as sports, executive, people carrier etc. Sports car drivers are likely to have different needs to people carrier drivers.

Benefits

Market segmentation helps businesses:

☑ carry out market research

☑ tailor products to customer needs

☑ target promotions at specific groups.

Worked example

target C-B

Explain **one** way in which effective marketing can help improve the products of a business. **(3 marks)**

If a business understands their customers' needs their products and services can be developed to meet these needs. This means that the products will be more attractive and desirable, leading to a greater number of sales.

Make sure that you:
- identify **one** way (for example, product development)
- explain how it will improve the business's products.

Now try this

target D-C

1 Which **one** of the following would most likely be considered an example of marketing a product? **(1 mark)**

   A ☐ Employing a new marketing executive

   B ☐ Repairing a machine

   C ☐ Making improvements to a service

   D ☐ Surveying customers

Do not equate marketing with advertising. Advertising is one way of making customers aware of a product or service but it is not the definition of marketing.

2 What is meant by the term 'marketing'? **(2 marks)**

target E-D

Market research

Market research is gathering information about customers, competitors and market trends by collecting primary and secondary data. This information is used to help a business make decisions. There are three stages in market research.

Planning and designing the research ⟩⟩	Doing the research ⟩⟩	Analysing the information
❓ What are the aims of the research?	❓ What are the time limits for the research?	❓ Did people make the same or different comments?
❓ What research techniques could you use?	❓ What is the sample size?	❓ Could you identify any trends in the data?
❓ Should you use primary or secondary, qualitative or quantitative data?		

Making decisions

After analysing the information from market research, a business might ask questions like these:

☑ Is the marketing mix appropriate?

☑ Does a product or service need to be changed to make it more appropriate for customers' needs?

☑ Should a product or service be left unchanged?

☑ Is it time to withdraw or replace a product or service?

Real life market research

When reading about market research in a case study, ask yourself the following questions:

• Was the right type of research used?

• How accurate is the research likely to be?

• Is the research representative of the target market?

• Is there any important information that the market research does not tell us?

This will help you discuss the likely success of a product or an idea.

Worked example

Apple produces home electronics, including strong brands like the iPod and iPhone, for the mass market. Product design is an important part of its success.

target B-A

Some other methods of collecting qualitative market research are interviews, consumer panels or questionnaires/surveys.

(a) Identify **one** method of collecting qualitative market research. **(1 mark)**

Focus groups

(b) Explain how qualitative market research might allow Apple to improve its marketing mix. **(3 marks)**

Qualitative research will give Apple information about whether consumers find their computers, iPads and iPhones attractive. This will enable Apple to change their product design so that consumers will pay more.

EXAM ALERT!

Only one in twenty students got all three marks for part **(b)**. Make sure you relate your answer to the case study, examining the effects on the business.

This was a real exam question that a lot of students struggled with – **be prepared!**

Now try this

target G-F

1 What is meant by the term 'market research'? **(2 marks)**

2 Identify **one** way in which a business might collect quantitative market research data. **(1 mark)**

3 Explain **one** way in which market research data might benefit a business. **(3 marks)**

target D-C

Product trial and repeat purchase

A PRODUCT TRIAL is when consumers buy a product for the first time to assess whether or not they want to buy it again. If this is successful, it could lead to REPEAT PURCHASES and CUSTOMER LOYALTY, where customers will buy a product more than once and keep coming back.

In this topic you should know:

☑ the range of methods a business could use to trial a product

☑ the range of methods to build customer loyalty and encourage repeat purchase

☑ how businesses might change their marketing activity over time.

Case studies

Different marketing techniques are suitable for different products. Product trial and repeat purchase marketing will be very different if a business is selling a chocolate bar or a car. Try to think of realistic and practical examples and apply them to the business in the case study.

Product trial

A business must get customers through the door so that they try the product for the first time. Methods used to do this might include:

Low trial prices — Advertising — Public relations — **Product trial** — Viral marketing, e.g. Facebook — Free samples

Repeat purchase and customer loyalty

Businesses aim to keep customers loyal, so that they make repeat purchases. This will generate sales and revenue. Methods that might be used to do this include:

☑ special promotions

☑ reminder adverts

☑ product innovations

☑ customer loyalty schemes (loyalty cards).

The cost of retaining existing customers can be less than that of attracting new ones.

Worked example

Subway is a well known sandwich retailer. It has become successful by offering consumers a choice and providing a healthier fast food option.

target C-B

Identify **two** different methods of 'product trial' that Subway could use.   **(2 marks)**

1 Press release   2 Free samples

Other possible answers might be:
- advertising
- publicity
- special offers
- viral marketing
- low trial prices.

You do not need to spend time writing long answers for 'identify' questions.

Now try this

In 2008, Pepsi launched its first major product since 1993. Pepsi Raw is a cola drink that is made from entirely natural ingredients and contains no artificial flavouring or sweeteners. The drink was launched in 2009 after a year of market research which saw a product trial take place in seven UK cities. Pepsi hope the new drink would allow it to catch up with its main rival, Coca-Cola, which was the market leader in the UK soft drinks market.

target C-B

1 What is meant by the term 'product trial'?   **(2 marks)**

target D-C

2 Explain **one** reason why Pepsi might want to create customer loyalty toward Pepsi Raw.   **(3 marks)**

41

Product life cycle 1

The product life cycle

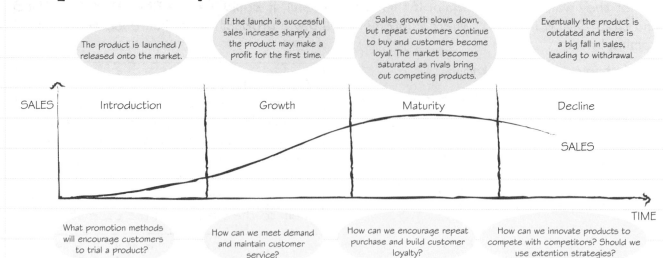

The product is launched / released onto the market.

If the launch is successful sales increase sharply and the product may make a profit for the first time.

Sales growth slows down, but repeat customers continue to buy and customers become loyal. The market becomes saturated as rivals bring out competing products.

Eventually the product is outdated and there is a big fall in sales, leading to withdrawal.

SALES — Introduction — Growth — Maturity — Decline

SALES

TIME

What promotion methods will encourage customers to trial a product?

How can we meet demand and maintain customer service?

How can we encourage repeat purchase and build customer loyalty?

How can we innovate products to compete with competitors? Should we use extention strategies?

Extension strategies

Businesses can increase the life of a product using extension strategies. This involves slightly changing the product so that it has a fresh appeal to the target market or appeals to a new market segment.

Think about how the product life cycle links all aspects of marketing together.

Worked example

(a) Identify **two** possible extension strategies that a chocolate manufacturer might use.   **(2 marks)**

1 Create new packaging.
2 Add new ingredients or flavours.

(b) Explain how **one** of the strategies you identified would extend the product life cycle of the new chocolate bar.   **(3 marks)**

Developing a new packaging for the chocolate bar could make it more eye-catching and therefore attract customer attention. As chocolate bars are often bought on impulse, this could help boost sales and revive the product.

EXAM ALERT!

Only one in twenty students got all three marks for the second part of the question. Make sure that you identify **one** way (for example, product development) and explain how it will improve the business's products. Remember to refer to **chocolate bars** in this answer.

This was a real exam question that a lot of students struggled with – **be prepared!**

Results Plus

Now try this

1 Identify the phase of the product life cycle sales where sales are likely to be rising most rapidly.
   Select **one** answer.   **(1 mark)**

   A ☐ Decline   C ☐ Maturity

   B ☐ Growth   D ☐ Development

2 Explain **one** reason why a business might use an extension strategy in the maturity phase of the product life cycle.
   (3 marks)

Product life cycle 2

Product portfolio analysis

Businesses sell a range of products. This is the PRODUCT MIX or PRODUCT PORTFOLIO. New products are constantly launched onto the market. Product portfolio analysis helps a business to make decisions about:

- what products to launch and when
- when to withdraw a product
- what products are doing well or badly now and in future
- how to increase sales.

The product life cycle and cash flow

Cash flow is the movement of money into and out of a business. Cash flow changes over the life of a product.

- INTRODUCTION phase – net cash flow is negative (more money goes out than comes in).
- GROWTH phase – net cash flow is positive but small (a little more comes in than goes out).
- MATURITY and DECLINE phases – at maturity, cash flow is likely to be positive; in decline, a business will start to experience cash-flow issues.

The Boston Matrix

The Boston Matrix is a product portfolio analysis tool used to plan the development of products. It can be closely linked to the product life cycle.

Star: very successful product, but growth has to be funded to keep up with demand and cash flow may be a problem.

Cash cow: little growth, but an established and profitable product that can support others.

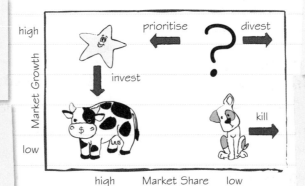

Question: presents a problem – should the business invest to increase sales?

Dog: few prospects, but should the business continue to sell it if it is profitable and it funds other products?

Worked example

target C-B

Describe how the Boston Matrix can benefit a business. **(3 marks)**

The Boston Matrix puts products into categories according to the growth rate and share of the market they have. It tells the business whether it has too many similar products or not and can help it to identify when it needs to withdraw products or introduce new ones.

EXAM ALERT!

Fewer than one in ten students got full marks for this question. You need to make three points about the benefits of the Boston Matrix to the business and you might include a definition or example.

This was a real exam question that a lot of students struggled with – **be prepared!**

 ResultsPlus

Now try this

target B-A

1 What is meant by the term 'product portfolio analysis'? **(2 marks)**

2 Explain **one** way in which managing a product portfolio can benefit a business. **(3 marks)**

Branding and differentiation

A BRAND is a named product which consumers see as being different from other products and which they can associate and identify with.

Branded products

- Consumers are more willing to trial products in the brand range.
- Brands encourage consumer loyalty.
- Consumers trust brands, leading to repeat purchases.
- Brands can often charge premium prices.
- Consumers have greater awareness of brands.
- Brands can lead to increased sales and market share.

Generic / non-branded products

- Very little difference between the product of one business compared to another. There is nothing to differentiate product by.

Market mapping

A MARKET MAP can show the difference between strongly branded products. This map shows the positions of cars in relation to their performance and practicality.

PRODUCT DIFFERENTIATION is about making a product different from others in some way. It helps businesses:

- to position their products and target different market segments
- to gain an advantage over rivals when faced with competition.

It allows consumers to see clearly that their needs are being met more effectively by one product than by another.

Differentiating a product

- Unique and catchy product name.
- Quality.
- Design, formulation or function.
- Packaging.
- Customer service.
- Differentiation across the value chain.

Worked example

target **E-D**

Describe **one** reason why it is important for Subway to differentiate its product. **(3 marks)**

As the fast-food market is very competitive it is important for Subway to stand out. Providing a healthier food option means that they can target a specific market segment and meet the needs of these customers better.

This answer includes a reason and there are two further relevant points of description. The question is based on a real business and the student has referred to the fast-food market in order to apply their answer.

Now try this

target **D-C**

target **E-D**

1 Identify **one** possible method a business could use to differentiate its brand. **(1 mark)**

2 Explain **one** reason why a strong brand might benefit a business. **(3 marks)**

Successful marketing mix 1

The MARKETING MIX is a combination of factors which help a business to take into account customer needs when selling a product.

The marketing mix is often referred to as the '4 Ps'.

Product   Price

Marketing mix

Promotion   Place

It is important that all aspects of the marketing mix complement each other and work together well. Just like baking a cake, it is important to get the right balance of ingredients.

1 The PRODUCT must meet the needs of the customer, and a business must consider the following when DIFFERENTIATING their product from others:

- Who is our product targeted at?
- What will be our product range (variety)?
- What will be our unique selling point (USP)?
- What will our brand be about / brand name be?
- What will be our formula (ingredients or materials)?
- What will our packaging be?

2 PRICE is important because:

- The price of a product gives customers an indication of quality.
- In competitive markets, changes in price can have a significant influence on demand.
- Branded products generally have a higher price than non-branded products because they are more expensive to produce and promote.

 £90

Luxury brands can charge a PREMIUM PRICE for their products.

The average price for a pair of trainers is £45. Some businesses will base their price on that of competitors.

£45

£20

A low price might be used by GENERIC / NON-BRANDED PRODUCTS or to encourage PRODUCT TRIAL when a product is first launched.

In 2009 Marks and Spencer faced falling sales. It wanted to maintain its profits and looked at either cutting prices or increasing advertising.

Which of these **two** methods do you think would be more effective in allowing Marks and Spencer to maintain its profits and why?   **(6 marks)**

...Overall, rather than cut prices M&S should do more advertising to boost customer visits. This will increase sales and therefore profits, although it might depend on the design and quality of the advertising, as it is not guaranteed to boost sales.

This is an extract from a student answer.

EXAM ALERT!

One in four students scored five or six marks for this question. You need to make sure that you relate your answer to Marks and Spencer and give a balanced view in your answer.

This was a real exam question that a lot of students struggled with – **be prepared!**   ResultsPlus

When answering this question you should give a judgement about both methods, with a clear reason why one is good and the other is not appropriate. Or you could make two points about the same issue.

Successful marketing mix 2

3 PROMOTION is the way in which a business makes consumers aware that a product is for sale. Reasons for promoting a business or product include:

- Creating awareness.
- Communicating product benefits and features to customers.
- Building a strong brand image.
- Boosting sales.

Methods of promotion

Advertising (including TV, magazines, radio, internet and billboards) is one method of promotion. Other methods include public relations (positive publicity) and sales promotions (special offers).

4 PLACE is about having a product available to customers when they want it and where they want it. There are a number of ways in which a business might do this.

- DIRECT – some businesses sell direct to customers. This process has been made more accessible with the growth of internet sales. A business may also employ a sales force to sell directly to customers.
- RETAIL – distributing products through retailers helps sell the product by improving the buying experience of customers and improving customer service.
- WHOLESALE – a wholesaler breaks down bulk supply of a product and distributes it to retailers. Wholesale is a suitable method for businesses that produce large quantities of a product.

Worked example

target D-C

Explain **one** reason why place is an important aspect of the marketing mix.

(3 marks)

If a business gets 'place' right they will make their products more accessible to customers. As a result it is likely that there will be greater customer awareness, which could lead to increased sales over time.

This answer includes a reason with two logical chains of development to score all three marks. As a specific business is not mentioned in the question, the answer does not need to refer to a specific context.

Now try this

target G-F

1 Amazon is an online retailer. Which **one** of the following elements of the marketing mix does the online element represent?
Select **one** answer.   **(1 mark)**

A ☐ Price   C ☐ Promotion

B ☐ Product   D ☐ Place

2 What is meant by the term 'premium price'?   **(2 marks)**

3 Explain **one** reason why a business might charge a premium price for its product.   **(3 marks)**

4 Describe how a business might benefit from carrying out effective promotion. **(4 marks)**

target D-C

Design and research development

The variables that contribute to a successful design are function, cost and appearance. In order for a business to successfully achieve this DESIGN MIX, it may carry out scientific research and development.

The scientific research process

Scientific research involves using scientific methods to develop new technologies, processes and materials for product invention and innovation.

Research and Development		Prototypes		Testing
Researching new technologies, techniques and processes for the development of products.		A working model of a possible finished product that can be trialled and tested.		Testing for safety and durability, and to collect market research information.

The design mix a product has can DIFFERENTIATE it from other products. For a laptop, the design mix may include the following:

- **Function.** This is about how well a product does what it is meant to. For a laptop this would include processing speed, memory and performance of the software.

- **Cost.** The cost is closely linked to price. Businesses will try to keep costs low, but improved functionality and appearance will increase cost. The better the technology and screen size, the more expensive the laptop will cost to produce.

- **Appearance.** Style and elegance are important for many products. Modern laptops can be found in multiple colours and continue to be designed thinner and lighter.

Worked example

target
D-C

> Marks and Spencer carries out research and development. One product that resulted from their research was a machine-washable wool suit that did not need to be dry cleaned.

Explain **one** benefit of research and development such as this to Marks and Spencer.   **(3 marks)**

Research and development will help a business like Marks and Spencer differentiate its products from competitors. Through R&D, Marks and Spencer was able to develop a new technology that other suit retailers do not have and therefore its products have a USP that cannot easily be copied.

EXAM ALERT!

One in six students got all three marks for this question. This student has given a reason ('differentiate its products') and then given two linked points of development. The answer is in the **context** of the case study: Marks and Spencer's machine-washable wool suits.

This was a real exam question that a lot of students struggled with – **be prepared!**

Now try this

target
A-A*

Using the case study in the worked example above, answer the following question.

1   In developing a machine-washable wool suit, Marks and Spencer had to consider both cost and function as part of their design mix. Which of these **two** elements do you believe is more important in helping Marks and Spencer produce a successful product?   **(6 marks)**

Managing stock 1

Managing STOCK is about managing the materials that a business holds in the most efficient and effective way. Stock can include materials waiting to be used in the production process, work in progress, and some can be finished stock waiting to be delivered to customers.

Bar gate stock

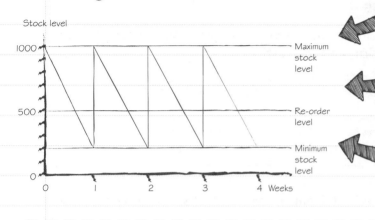

The MAXIMUM STOCK LEVEL the business is able to hold.

The RE-ORDER LEVEL is the point at which new stock will be ordered by the business. The difference between this level and the point at which stock increases is the time it takes for the stock to arrive.

Also known as BUFFER STOCK. The MINIMUM STOCK LEVEL is the lowest amount of stock the business will hold. It is a safety net in case there is a surge in demand.

Just In Time stock control

JUST IN TIME (JIT) stock control is a stock management system where stock is delivered only when it is needed by the production system, and so no stock is kept by a business. For JIT to work a business must have good relationships with suppliers, a well-organised production system, and regular demand for their products.

January						
Monday	Tuesday	Wednesday	Thursday	Friday	Saturday	Sunday
2	3	4	5	6	7	8
9 Order placed	10 Stock arrives	11 Product made	12 →	13	14 Product distributed to customer	15
16	17	18	19	20	21	22

Worked example

target C-B

The diagram illustrates the bar gate stock graph for Go-Go Hamsters at the Saltash Toy Box.

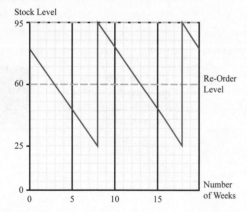

Use the diagram to calculate how many weeks it will take for stock of Go-Go Hamsters to arrive at the Saltash Toy Box after re-ordering.   **(2 marks)**

Stock is ordered in week 3 and arrives in week 8. Therefore 8 – 3 = 5 weeks.

EXAM ALERT!

Fewer than four in ten students got this question wrong. Always show your calculations. If you make an error you can still pick up one mark if your calculations show that you understand how to calculate the answer.

This was a real exam question that a lot of students struggled with – **be prepared!**

Now try this

target D-C

1 Using the diagram in the worked example, identify the number of Go-Go Hamsters the Saltash Toy Box holds as a buffer stock.   **(1 mark)**

2 What is meant by the term 'just in time stock control'?   **(2 marks)**

Managing stock 2

A business can choose between using a 'JUST IN CASE' stock control system or a 'JUST IN TIME' stock control system. Just In Time is usually more appropriate for large manufacturers, although it will depend on demand and the nature of the product and production methods. Just In Case involves having a backup of stock at all times.

Benefits of holding stock:

- ☑ Businesses can meet unpredicted surges in demand.
- ☑ Businesses can replace damaged goods.
- ☑ A business can receive discounts for bulk buying.
- ☑ Limited problems.

Benefits of holding little or no stock:

- ☑ Cost saving in not having to store stock.
- ☑ Less chance of damaged or stolen stock.
- ☑ Employees can focus on tasks other than managing stock.
- ☑ Can reduce costs of production, which makes product pricing more competitive.

Worked example

target
C-B

As a result of the decision to close its store, the Saltash Toy Box changed the way it held stock. It now uses a just-in-time (JIT) method of stock control.

State **one** advantage and **one** disadvantage to the Saltash Toy Box of adopting a just-in-time (JIT) method of stock control. For each, explain **one** likely effect on the business. **(8 marks)**

Advantage: Lower cost

Explanation: If Saltash Toy Box uses JIT it saves money on storage costs. This money could then go towards promoting its Go-Go Hamsters and this could lead to an increased number of sales.

Disadvantage:

Explanation:

This is an extract from a student answer.

EXAM ALERT!

Only one in twelve students got seven or eight marks for this question. This type of question is split into two 'identify' and two 'explain' questions. Make sure you explain the advantage **and** disadvantage you have identified and relate your answer to Saltash Toy Box.

This was a real exam question that a lot of students struggled with – **be prepared!**   Results Plus

Now try this

target
G-F

1. What is meant by the term 'stock'? **(2 marks)**

target
F-E

2. Explain **one** possible disadvantage to Saltash Toy Box of holding a large stock of toys. **(3 marks)**

Managing quality

Two ways of achieving good quality in business is through QUALITY CONTROL and QUALITY ASSURANCE.

- QUALITY CONTROL is seen as one part of the chain of production. A quality controller will examine and / or test for quality once a product has been made.

- QUALITY ASSURANCE involves focusing on quality at every stage of the production process. Everyone is involved and is responsible for contributing towards the achievement of a quality standard. As a result, there should be zero defects.

The benefits of good quality

☑ Good quality allows for a premium price to be charged.

☑ Good quality builds a strong brand image.

☑ Good quality is closely linked to meeting customer needs.

☑ Quality is a way of differentiating a product.

Another benefit of quality is less waste as there are fewer faulty products.

Quality assurance checklist

For a business to have a quality assurance system it must:

☑ have quality as the focus of every process

☑ involve customers and suppliers at the design stage

☑ aim for zero defects

☑ have quality as the responsibility of every employee

☑ have managers who ensure there are systems in place to assure quality

☑ meet a QUALITY STANDARD, such as ISO 9000

☑ make good quality part of the culture, something everyone aims for and is involved in.

Worked example

target
A–A*

Having a quality control system or a quality culture are two ways a business might try to improve quality.

Which of these two do you think would be more successful in improving quality in a business such as Go-Go Hamsters, and why?   **(6 marks)**

...Overall, a quality culture is the best approach because quality is guaranteed at every stage of the production process. The success of this approach may depend on how well employees are trained in delivering quality standards in their work.

In this part of the answer the student is writing about quality culture and finishes with a conclusion. The answer shows balance by following the 'it depends' rule.

Remember that there is no right or wrong answer about which approach is more successful but you need to **justify** your choice.

This is an extract from a student answer.

Now try this

1   Explain **one** benefit for a business of producing high-quality products.   **(3 marks)**

target
E–D

Cost-effective operations and competitiveness

Increasing productivity

PRODUCTIVTY is output per worker. It measures how much each worker produces over a period of time. It can be calculated using the formula:

total output ÷ number of workers

Increasing productivity leads to greater competitiveness in a market. Productivity can be improved by increasing output or by lowering the costs of production (inputs) while maintaining output.

Methods of increasing output

- ✓ Train employees better.
- ✓ Invest in better equipment.
- ✓ Introduce more effective work practices.
- ✓ Work overtime.
- ✓ Motivate employees.

Competitive prices

Cost-effective operations can help businesses to lower prices and be competitive against rivals.

Increased productivity

⬇

Lower costs

⬇

Lower prices

⬇

Attract more customers

⬇

Increased sales and profits

Methods of reducing costs

- ✓ Improved purchasing (cheaper suppliers).
- ✓ Better design of products.
- ✓ Cheaper labour costs.
- ✓ Cutting overhead costs.
- ✓ Streamline the production process.
- ✓ Relocation.

Worked example

target C-B

1 What is meant by the term 'competitiveness'? **(2 marks)**

Competitiveness is where a firm has some kind of advantage over a rival firm, such as higher productivity, that will allow it to gain customers from rivals.

This answer has gained a mark for highlighting an advantage and another for giving an example.

2 Explain one benefit to Sony of improving its productivity. **(3 marks)**

By increasing productivity Sony can make more products per hour, such as Sony PlayStations. This will reduce the costs of making each product. Reducing costs could allow Sony to lower its prices and gain sales from rivals.

This student has achieved all three marks by giving a benefit and then giving two points of development. The answer is in the context of the case study, as it refers to Sony.

Now try this

target G-F

1 Identify **two** methods a business can use to reduce costs. **(2 marks)**

target A-A*

2 Improving the quality of a product and improving productivity are two ways in which a business such as McDonald's might become more competitive. Which of these **two** methods do you think would be most effective in improving the competitiveness of a business such as McDonald's and why? **(6 marks)**

Effective customer service

Effective customer service checklist

☑ Meet and exceed needs of customers.
☑ Provide high-quality products and services.
☑ Innovation (keep moving forward).
☑ Spot problems and potential problems.
☑ Listen to customers.
☑ Deal effectively and quickly with complaints.
☑ Be on time.
☑ Train staff in customer service.

The drawbacks of poor customer service

☒ Poor customer satisfaction.
☒ Poor brand image.
☒ Inability to differentiate a product and gain a competitive advantage.
☒ Inability to charge a premium price.
☒ Fall in sales and profits. Sales changing to rival products.
☒ Fall in repeat purchase and customer loyalty.

Worked example

target **A-A***

Jason and Balvir will seek to increase their competitive advantage when they open their restaurant. Assess how improved customer service could help them achieve this. **(8 marks)**

Improved customer service will help Jason and Balvir deliver a better dining experience for their customers. Experience and service is an important aspect of eating out and this could lead to customer loyalty and repeat purchase. Considering that there are almost 7000 restaurants in London it may also help them differentiate their business. Alternatively, delivering high levels of customer service requires training and employing the best employees. This could be expensive for a new business...

This part of the student's answer makes reference to two effects of delivering improved customer service. The student has not presumed that introducing improved customer service will automatically or inevitably lead to competitive advantage and has discussed both the advantages and disadvantages of the option. Make sure you also:

• Include a justified conclusion based on your analysis.
• Use the 'it depends' rule to show balance.
• Answer in the **context** of Jason and Balvir's new restaurant business.

This is an extract from a student answer.

Now try this

target **B-A**

1 What is meant by the term 'effective customer service'? **(2 marks)**

target **F-D**

2 (a) Identify **two** drawbacks to a business of poor customer service. **(2 marks)**

(b) For **one** method you have identified in (a), explain how this may affect the business. **(3 marks)**

Consumer protection laws

The Sale of Goods Act

This relates to the products and services being sold by businesses.
All products must:
- ✓ be of merchantable quality
- ✓ match their description
- ✓ be fit for purpose.

The Trade Descriptions Act

This relates to how businesses deal with and sell to customers.
All businesses must not:
- ✗ give false information
- ✗ fail to give (withhold) important information
- ✗ act aggressively (force the sale).

Impact of consumer protection laws

Drawbacks

- Businesses must know the law and keep up to date.
- Laws can restrict businesses from operating as they would wish.
- Businesses have to comply with laws by changing their products and practices and this can be costly.
- Bad publicity if not followed.

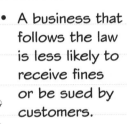
Drawbacks
Benefits

Benefits

- A business that follows the law is less likely to receive fines or be sued by customers.
- Meeting consumer protection laws can improve a business's image.
- Improved relationship with stakeholders.
- Good publicity is followed.

> The topic of consumer protection law is closely linked to ethics in business. A business that closely adheres to the law is also acting ethically and may benefit from this.

Worked example

target
A-A*

Using your knowledge of consumer protection laws, is Pepsi right to use the words 'raw' and 'natural' in relation to its new product? **(10 marks)**

...Ultimately it depends on how honest Pepsi are about their advertising of new products and whether customers feel that they are acting ethically. This type of language is used all the time by drinks manufacturers and most consumers will understand that a soft drink is never going to be as healthy as water. Therefore, Pepsi is not really doing anything wrong by using these phrases because the consumers are not being misled and no consumer protection laws are being breached.

Make sure you:
- develop both sides of the argument
- use your understanding of consumer protection law
- make a judgement with clear justification.

The last part of this answer has made good use of the 'it depends' rule to show balance in the conclusion.

This is an extract from a student answer.

Now try this

target
E-D

1 Identify **one** consumer protection law that a business will have to adhere to.   **(1 mark)**

target
C-B

2 (a) Identify **one** disadvantage to a business of the government introducing new consumer protection legislation.   **(1 mark)**
   (b) Explain how this could affect the business.   **(3 marks)**

Improving cash flow

Managing cash flow

FINANCIAL MANAGEMENT is about changing monetary variables such as cash flows to achieve financial objectives such as improved cash flow.

INFLOW ➤ | BUSINESS
Keep cash in
the business | OUTFLOW ➤

Speed it up / increase　　　　Slow it down / reduce

Why is cash important?

A business can still be profitable but run out of cash. If a business's outflows are greater than its inflows (or the outflows occur at a faster rate) then it could run out of cash and trading will cease.

Improving cash outflows

- Delay paying invoices.
- Leasing rather than buying.
- Reduce stock orders.
- Improve credit terms with suppliers.
- Use cheaper suppliers.

Improving cash inflows

- Increasing sales revenue.
- De-stocking.
- Reduce credit terms with customers.
- Encourage customers to pay early (incentives).
- Use short-term sources of finance, e.g. overdrafts and short-term loans.

Worked example

1　Identify **two** possible ways Lidl could improve its cash flow. **(2 marks)**

1　Lease rather than buy assets.
2　De-stocking.

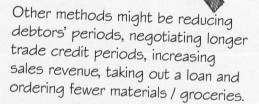

Other methods might be reducing debtors' periods, negotiating longer trade credit periods, increasing sales revenue, taking out a loan and ordering fewer materials / groceries.

2　Explain **one** reason why strong cash flow is important to a supermarket such as Lidl. **(3 marks)**

Lidl requires a strong cash flow as it wants to expand the number of stores. With a strong cash flow Lidl is less likely to default on payments and therefore be able to cover any costs associated with the expansion.

You must make reference to the supermarket / food context.

Now try this

1　Which of the following is a cash inflow? Select **one** answer. **(1 mark)**

　A ☐ Payments to suppliers
　B ☐ Purchasing assets
　C ☐ Longer credit terms for customers
　D ☐ Taking out a bank loan

2　Identify **two** reasons why a business might want to establish more favourable credit terms with suppliers. **(2 marks)**

Improving profit

Improving profit is not easy

Techniques to raise revenue or cut costs can affect the performance of the business and in the long-term this could reduce profits. For example:

- Cutting material costs ⇨ lower quality products
- Cutting labour costs ⇨ lower motivation of workforce
- Cutting investment ⇨ damages long-term competitiveness
- Improve products ⇨ expensive development costs
- Increase prices ⇨ customers switch to competitors' products

Improving profit

To improve profits a business can focus on two areas: increasing revenue or lowering costs.

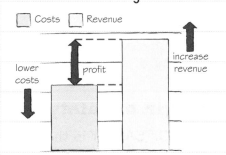

Increasing revenues

NUMBER OF PRODUCTS SOLD × AVERAGE PRICE = TOTAL REVENUE

A business could increase revenues through:

- improved marketing
- better products
- increasing its selling price.

Any business increasing its price has to be very careful. The impact an increase in price has on revenue depends on how sensitive demand is to a change in price.

Cutting costs

FIXED COSTS + VARIABLE COSTS = TOTAL COSTS

A business could reduce its costs by:

- cutting costs of raw materials, labour or research and development costs
- cutting its marketing.

Outline **one** method a business might use to increase its profits.   **(3 marks)**

A business could increase advertising. This could lead to greater awareness and interest in their products and therefore more revenue through sales.

EXAM ALERT!

Fewer than one in four students got all three marks for this question. The command word here is **outline**. You need to identify a method of increasing profit and then make two points in relation to the method identified.

This was a real exam question that a lot of students struggled with – **be prepared!**

ResultsPlus

Now try this

target
C–B

1   Identify **one** problem a business might face if it made a loss.   **(1 mark)**

Jason and Balvir are setting up a new restaurant business in London. Jason believes that he should charge a price of £35 for the set menu. Balvir thinks £30 would be a more appropriate price.

2   In your opinion, which price would be more likely to help the business to survive the first year? Justify your answer.   **(8 marks)**

Break-even charts

VARIABLE COSTS, e.g. materials, change directly with the number of products made.

The point on the graph where total costs and revenue meet is the BREAK-EVEN POINT.

When TOTAL REVENUE is above the break-even point the business makes a PROFIT. Below it, it makes a LOSS.

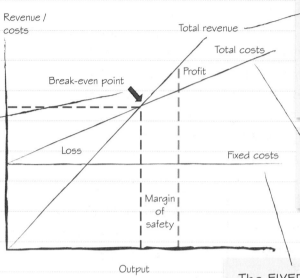

Revenue / costs

Total revenue

Total costs

Profit

Break-even point

Loss

Fixed costs

Margin of safety

Output

TOTAL REVENUE is the amount of money earned by a business from selling products. It increases directly with the number of products sold.

TOTAL COSTS are the sum of all the costs at any level of output.

The FIXED COSTS line is horizontal. Fixed costs, e.g. rent, do not change at any level of output.

Formulas to know

Total revenue = quantity sold × average price

Total costs = fixed cost + variable cost

Break even = fixed costs ÷ contribution

CONTRIBUTION is a price per item – variable cost per item.

The margin of safety

The MARGIN OF SAFETY is the amount of output between the actual level of output where profit is being made and the break-even level of output. This is how much production could fall before the business starts to make a loss.

target C-B

Sony's fixed costs for the PlayStation 3 are £2 400 000 and variable costs are £140 per console.

Calculate the break-even point when the PlayStation 3 was priced at £300. Show your working and the formula used.   **(3 marks)**

Break even = Total fixed costs ÷ Price – variable cost per item.

Break even = £2 400 000 ÷ £300 – £140

Break even = 15 000 consoles

Make sure you:
- show a correct formula
- show accurate workings
- calculate the correct answer.

target E-D

1   What is meant by the term 'break-even point'?   **(2 marks)**

target D-C

Sony's fixed costs for the PlayStation 3 are £2 400 000 and variable costs are £140 per console.

2   Calculate the level of profit or loss Sony would make if it sold 20 000 PlayStation 3 consoles at £300 each.   **(3 marks)**

Break-even analysis

Break-even analysis is a useful tool to help a business make decisions and set targets, and plan for the future.

Break-even analysis is a useful tool for answering 'what if?' questions such as: what would be the impact of an increase in variable costs on profit? Any fall in fixed or variable costs is likely to lower the break-even point. An increase in price will also lower the number of units required to break even.

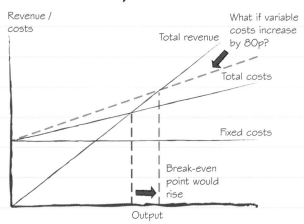

Lowering the break-even point

Break-even analysis can identify strategies for lowering the break-even point and increasing profit.

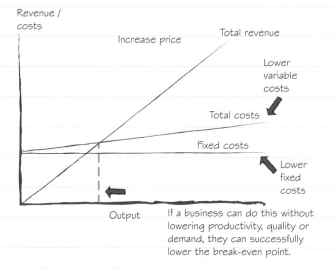

If a business can do this without lowering productivity, quality or demand, they can successfully lower the break-even point.

Caution! The concept of break-even assumes that a business will sell all the products it makes. In reality, if a business increases price it will lower the break-even point, but this might deter customers from buying the more expensive product.

Using break-even analysis

A business might use break-even when:

- understanding the past (were past decisions on price correct?)
- setting and achieving production targets
- launching a new product
- starting a new business
- developing a business plan.

Worked example

target **B-A**

Explain the relevance of margin of safety to Jason and Balvir's restaurant business. **(3 marks)**

Jason and Balvir's restaurant needs to have a considerable margin of safety because sales could easily fall in a competitive market like the restaurant market. Falling below the margin of safety would lead to a loss and therefore the business could struggle to survive.

This answer gives a reason why the margin of safety is important to the business. Two logical chains of explanation are developed in **context** by referring to the 'competitive restaurant market'.

Now try this

target **C-B**

A business is using a break-even chart to examine the effect of a reduction in the price of its product.

1. Identify **one** problem a business may face as a result of reducing the price. **(1 mark)**

2. Explain how the problem you have identified in question 1 would affect the business. **(3 marks)**

Financing growth

A business can use INTERNAL (from within the business) or EXTERNAL (from outside the business) sources of funds to finance growth.

How can a business finance growth?

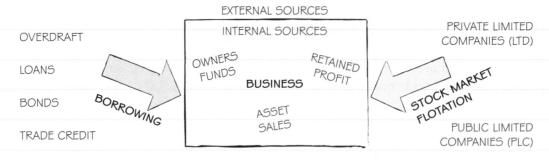

EXTERNAL SOURCES

INTERNAL SOURCES

OVERDRAFT

LOANS

BONDS

TRADE CREDIT

BORROWING

OWNERS FUNDS

BUSINESS

RETAINED PROFIT

ASSET SALES

STOCK MARKET FLOTATION

PRIVATE LIMITED COMPANIES (LTD)

PUBLIC LIMITED COMPANIES (PLC)

Comparing sources of finance

- RISK. Selling shares may mean owners lose control, or cash-flow problems may result from meeting loan-repayment terms.
- COST. The cost of borrowing varies across different sources.
- AVAILABILITY. Some sources, such as loans or share capital, might not be accessible.

Questions to consider

When choosing sources of finance a business should consider:

1 Is it a short-term or long-term requirement?

2 How much finance is required?

3 If we borrow it how much will it cost (interest rate %)?

4 What sources are available to our business?

5 What level of debt can we manage?

Worked example

target
D–C

Explain **one** disadvantage to the business of borrowing money from a bank to finance growth.   **(3 marks)**

If a business borrows money from a bank it has to repay the loan on a fixed-term basis with interest. A business could then struggle to make these regular payments and this could lead to cash-flow problems.

EXAM ALERT!

Fewer than one in twenty students got all three marks for this question. This student has given a clear drawback of using a loan to finance growth. They have then developed two logical chains of argument identifying the knock-on effect of this: the struggle to make payments and cash-flow problems. Make sure your answer refers to **borrowing money from a bank**.

This was a real exam question that a lot of students struggled with – **be prepared!**   ResultsPlus

Now try this

target
C–B

target
G–F

1 Identify **one** internal source of finance that a business might use to expand.   **(1 mark)**

2 Explain **one** benefit to a business of the internal source of finance identified in question 1.   **(3 marks)**

Organisational structure

Organisational structure is the way in which a business is structured to achieve its objectives. This is normally through a HIERARCHY. A hierarchy is a structure of different levels of authority in a business organisation, one on top of the other.

Organisational structure

A business can be organised in a number of ways.

Product divisions

Regional divisions

Functional areas such as marketing or finance

Organisation charts

Organisational structures can be shown through organisation charts.

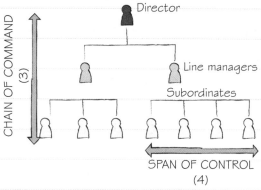

LINE MANAGERS can pass on authority to their SUBORDINATES through DELEGATION.

Centralised or decentralised?

- Centralised decisions are made by senior managers (normally at head office).
- Decentralised decisions are delegated to regional employees at local stores and branches.

Centralised	Decentralised
Increased control and standardisation	Decisions devolved to branches or divisions that may know their local customers better
Decisions can be slow	Loss of control

Size

As businesses expand they will naturally employ more people, increasing the CHAIN OF COMMAND and SPAN OF CONTROL. The size and structure of an organisation can have an impact on communication, control and flexibility of a business.

A business can DOWNSIZE (reduce size) or DELAYER (reduce the number of layers in the hierarchy) to:

- reduce costs
- improve efficiency
- improve communication.

Worked example

target B-A

Explain **one** reason why a business might choose to delayer the organisation.   **(3 marks)**

Delayering can reduce costs and unnecessary employees. As a result the organisation could operate more efficiently and this could lead to increased profitability.

You need to give a clear benefit of delayering and then develop two arguments about the knock-on effect of this (such as operate more efficiently and increase profitability).

Now try this

target C-B

target D-C

1   What is meant by the term 'empowerment'?   **(2 marks)**

2   Explain **one** drawback of a business having a wide span of control. **(3 marks)**

Motivation theory

A motivated workforce

Motivation can lead to:

- a hard-working and flexible workforce, that is willing to 'go the extra mile' for the business
- greater commitment to the organisation
- less time off with illness
- improved customer service
- improved communication within the business.

Maslow's hierarchy of needs

Maslow suggested that people are motivated by five needs. In theory, people are driven to meet these needs in order, starting with physiological needs. How can they be used in the workplace?

Self-actualisation — Creating job opportunities, promotion and training to allow employees to achieve their potential.

Self-esteem — Creating promotion opportunities, empowering employees, using rewards to recognise the achievements of employees.

Love and belonging — Organising the workforce into teams, creating opportunities for employees to socialise.

Safety — Ensuring long-term progression and job security.

Physiological — Providing a clean and safe working environment and well-paid jobs.

Worked example

target A-A*

Sony's PlayStation 3 console has struggled against strong competition from Nintendo's Wii. Sony expects to make a loss of over £680 million in 2009. To combat this Sony plans to cut 8000 jobs and close several factories.

Assess the impact of factory closures on the motivation of the remaining Sony employees.   **(8 marks)**

The job losses at Sony are likely to reduce the motivation of employees, as many friendships will be affected. This could impact on employees' love-and-belonging needs. Further, employees' safety needs could be compromised as those that remain may doubt their job security. On the other hand, with fewer employees, there may be opportunities for promotion. This could help employees meet their higher-order needs. Ultimately...

In this extract the student has considered two different perspectives and used motivation theory to answer the question. The student clearly understands Maslow's hierarchy of needs and has used the theory to answer the question. The evaluation effectively uses the 'it depends' rule to show that other issues could affect motivation.

This is an extract from a student answer.

Now try this

target D-C

1   Identify **three** factors that could improve the motivation of workers in a business.   **(3 marks)**

2   Explain **one** benefit to a business of improved worker motivation.   **(3 marks)**

target F-D

Communication

The communication process

For communication to be effective:

- the SENDER has to choose an appropriate MEDIUM to reach the RECEIVER
- FEEDBACK should also be available to ensure the communication has been successful.

INSUFFICIENT or EXCESSIVE communication can have an impact on:

- employee motivation
- customer service
- the number of mistakes made
- the understanding of employees
- speed and implementation of decisions
- the image / brand of the business (through advertising).

Types of communication

FORMAL COMMUNICATION is approved by the organisation. It lays down rules of communication within a business.

INFORMAL COMMUNICATION (also known as 'the grapevine') is also used in business, such as gossip. It can get in the way of effective communication.

Barriers to effective communication

- Using inappropriate mediums or email system failure.
- Being angry or tired.
- Cultural differences.
- Use of jargon. This depends on the skill or knowledge of the sender or receiver.

Worked example

target **A-A***

Affinity is a small publishing company that produces guide books for walks. Using your knowledge of business, assess the importance of good communication to a company such as Affinity. **(10 marks)**

This is an extract from a student answer.

Poor communication could lead to lack of control and motivation of the workforce. If the company is expanding, it is likely to find communication difficult as it grows and new employees are introduced... Without effective formal communication channels sales could fall and this is a threat to the future of the business. This is perhaps more important than the problems of remuneration and motivation... The importance of communication at Affinity may depend on ...

EXAM ALERT!

Only three in ten students scored more than four marks for this question. You need to **assess** the importance of good communication in the small business context of Affinity. To do this you should discuss at least two reasons using the appropriate business terminology, show balance in your answer, make a judgement and give clear justification for your judgement.

This was a real exam question that a lot of students struggled with – **be prepared!**   Results**Plus**

Now try this

1. Identify **two** barriers to communication in a business. **(2 marks)**
2. Describe how **one** of these barriers can affect the communication process. **(3 marks)**

target **C-B**

Remuneration

REMUNERATION is the payments system adopted by a business to pay and reward employees.

Time-based systems	Salaries	Results-based systems (suitable where output or success can be measured)	Fringe benefits
Wages for part-time or full-time workers	For non-manual jobs	Piece rates	Company car
Overtime	For professional workers	Commission	Healthcare
		Bonus schemes	Pension schemes
			Company discounts

Types of worker

- Part-time workers
- Full-time workers
- Temporary workers
- Freelance workers (self-employed)
- Manual workers (Blue collar)
- Non-manual (White collar)

Different types of employees will require different types of payment systems to ensure they are motivated and paid fairly.

A business will often use a variety of remuneration methods to motivate and get the best out of its employees. Think what methods could be combined for best effect.

Choosing a payment system

The following things can influence the choice of payment system:

- Nature of the job – a piece-rate system might not fit the job of a secretary.
- Cost – a business will choose the most cost-effective option.
- Motivation – pay, as we have seen, is closely linked to employee motivation.
- Flexibility – a business might pay a one-off fee to a consultant so that they do not have to pay them over a long period.

Different payment systems motivate workers in different ways. For example, a commission system will motivate sales staff to sell more. Choosing the right payment system will maximise the output of workers. The wrong system could waste money.

Worked example

target D-C

Identify **two** other methods of remuneration, apart from salary and payment by the hour, that a business could use to reward employees. **(2 marks)**

1 Piece rate
2 Commission

EXAM ALERT!

Fewer than six in ten students got both marks for this question. Other possible answers include:

- fringe benefits (extra holiday, company car)
- shares in the company.

Remember that remuneration is a **payments system** so promotion is not a method of remuneration.

This was a real exam question that a lot of students struggled with – **be prepared!** ResultsPlus

Now try this

target C-B

1 Explain **one** benefit to a business of rewarding workers using a 'piece rate' method of payment. **(3 marks)**

target B-A

2 Discuss the importance of increasing wages as a method of motivating workers employed in low-skilled industries. **(6 marks)**

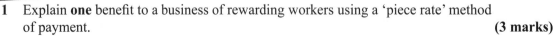

Ethics in business

Should a business:
– supply firms that are not ethical
– focus on the lowest costs or provide the best value to customers
– replenish the resources it uses / recycle
– sell products that damage customers' health
– do more for the local community other than providing jobs
– pay the lowest price possible to suppliers
– only use ethical suppliers?

Is paying the minimum wage fair?

Is it right to collaborate with competitors to keep prices high?

How much waste should it produce and how should it dispose of waste safely?

Profits or ethics?

A TRADE-OFF is when something is given up in order to gain or achieve something else. Is there a trade-off between profits and ethical behaviour?

Is this correct? Acting ethically can lower business profits. Paying higher wages, recycling and only using ethical suppliers is likely to raise costs and lower profits.

Or is this? Acting ethically can be appealing to customers and can motivate employees. This may lead to higher productivity and more sales, which will balance the cost of ethical policies.

Pressure groups

PRESSURE GROUPS are organisations that try to get businesses to change what they are doing. Pressure groups focus on issues such as animal rights, workers' rights, the environment and world poverty. Pressure groups can cause bad publicity for businesses that act unethically, which can damage their reputation.

Pressure group activity

Pressure group methods include lobbying, protests, working with businesses, refusing to work with businesses and boycotting products.

Worked example

target
C-B

Explain **one** way in which a business such as Tesco might be affected by a successful pressure-group campaign.
(3 marks)

A pressure-group campaign could show Tesco in a negative light and therefore damage the reputation or brand of the company. As a result, this could cost Tesco a lot of money and effort trying to rebuild their brand image.

EXAM ALERT!

Fewer than one in four students got all three marks for this answer. You need to **explain** how a company such as Tesco is affected by a pressure group.

This was a real exam question that a lot of students struggled with – **be prepared!**

ResultsPlus

Now try this

target
E-D

1 Identify **one** method a pressure group could use to persuade a business to act responsibly. **(1 mark)**

2 Identify **two** advantages to a business such as Tesco acting ethically. **(2 marks)**

target
D-C

Environmental issues

Most business operations will have an impact on the ENVIRONMENT in the short-term and long-term. All businesses have to manage this in order to achieve long-term success.

Environmental effects

Short-term effects	Long-term effects
Traffic congestion through transport and deliveries	Climate change
Air, noise and water pollution through manufacturing and industry	Depletion of land, food and natural resources

> The environmental impact of a business is closely linked to its growth. As businesses expand they will normally have a bigger impact on the environment.

Recycling is one way of reducing the environmental impact of business.

Other ways include:

* use of renewable energy
* replenishment and conservation of natural resources
* bio-degradable packaging
* reduction in food miles
* social enterprise.

Business opportunities

As consumers are becoming more environmentally aware, there is an opportunity for businesses to differentiate their products to meet customer needs and make them 'greener', e.g. the development of hybrid cars. There are also growing opportunities for businesses in 'green' industries, such as energy conservation and solar power.

Worked example

target
A-A*

In response to the work of the WWF, retailers of tuna could respond in one of the following two ways:
option 1: do nothing, or option 2: sell tuna caught only in an environmentally friendly way.

In your opinion which **one** of these two options should retailers adopt, and why?   **(6 marks)**

...Overall, it may depend on what other competitors are doing. If this becomes standard practice across the industry, all retailers will have to do this. Option 2 is the better option because it will improve sales in the long-term, counteracting any cost of switching.

In this question you need to:

* analyse an argument for option I and another for option 2, **OR**
* give advantages for one and a disadvantage for another, or the benefits of just one option.

The conclusion in this extract makes good use of the 'it depends' rule. An effective judgement has been made explaining why option 2 is better than option I.

This is an extract from a student answer.

Now try this

1 Identify **two** impacts a business might have on the environment.   **(2 marks)**

2 Explain **one** way that a business can limit the impact it has on the environment.   **(3 marks)**

Economic issues affecting international trade

Factors influencing trade

There is a range of factors that influence opportunities for international trade:

- How developed each country is (including income, wages and the quality and technology of products).
- Government regulations on imports and exports (including import protection, QUOTAS and export SUBSIDIES).

Developing countries and opportunities for UK businesses

- Lower costs of production in developing countries.
- Products cheaper when bought from abroad and then sold in the UK.
- The import of cheap natural resources.
- Increased demand from foreign markets as countries develop.

Developing countries may also be a threat to UK businesses, i.e. if the UK buys cheap imports, then UK businesses may suffer.

Policies affecting international trade

Governments can encourage international trade by supporting exports, or can restrict imports in order to protect their home markets.

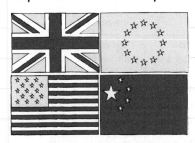

- Tariffs and customs duties tax imports and make them more expensive.
- Quotas put a limit on the number of imports.
- An export subsidy will reduce the price of exports and encourage exporting firms.
- Whether importing or exporting UK businesses may suffer or benefit from these policies.

Worked example

target A–A*

The UK has recently seen a significant rise in international trade with India due to economic developments and a rise in average incomes.

State **one** advantage and **one** disadvantage to a growth in international trade with India. **(8 marks)**

Advantage:

Explanation:

Disadvantage: Increased competition.

Explanation: As the Indian economy develops, their industries will become more competitive. This could lead to Indian firms entering the UK market and therefore reducing the market share and sales of UK firms who sell to UK consumers.

When answering this type of question you need to:
- give one advantage **and** one disadvantage
- give an explanation of **each**, with three clear logical chains of development.

This is an extract from a student answer.

Now try this

target C–B

1   What is meant by the term 'tariff'?
     (2 marks)

target B–A

2   What is meant by the term 'export subsidy'?
     (2 marks)

Government and the EU

The UK government and EU laws govern the way businesses in the UK operate, trade and deal with customers. Government intervention aims to encourage competition, help businesses run efficiently and protect consumers and employees.

EU regulations

Government and EU regulations include:

- accounting regulations
- the Trade Descriptions Act
- health and safety laws
- the minimum wage
- maternity and paternity rights.

Businesses will often take measures to avoid government intervention. For example:

- moving to a country such as Ireland, where corporation tax is lower
- producing products in countries with a lower minimum wage
- selling products in countries with relaxed health and safety laws.

Taxation

Examples of government taxation include:

- Value Added Tax (VAT)
- Corporation Tax
- Income Tax
- National Insurance (NI)

Taxation can affect consumers and businesses.

Taxes high

Consumers spend less ⇧
Consumers
⇩ Consumers spend more

Profits and dividends fall ⇧
Businesses
⇩ Profits and dividends rise

Taxes low

Regulations

Different regulations have benefits and drawbacks for business. The short-term impact of government regulation on businesses is to increase costs In the long-term it should make them more competitive and ethical.

	Benefits	Drawbacks
Minimum wage	Small businesses are able to compete with big businesses who might force down wage rates	Higher costs of labour will reduce profits
Maternity and paternity rights	Better relationships with employees and work-life balance	Working days lost while employee on maternity / paternity leave
Health and safety regulations	Fewer work-related accidents and injuries	Costs of health and safety regulations can hinder productivity

Worked example

target A-A*

Using your knowledge of business, assess whether it is right for the government to increase the national minimum wage to £5.80 per hour.   **(10 marks)**

...The extent to which increasing the minimum wage has a positive or negative impact depends on the current level of taxation. If taxes are already high it will have little impact on workers and put further pressure on businesses. Higher wages are ultimately a good thing because it will improve the fortunes of workers and this will then boost demand for businesses.

◄ This is an extract from a student answer.

EXAM ALERT!

Fewer than one in ten students scored between eight and ten marks for this question. The answer should contain an analysis of the positive and negative impact on UK businesses and their workers.

This was a real exam question that a lot of students struggled with – **be prepared!**   Result Plus

Now try this

target C-B

1 Identify **two** EU regulations that might affect UK businesses.   **(2 marks)**

2 Explain **one** benefit to a business of the UK being part of the European Union.   **(3 marks)**

Exam skills 1

You will have 1 hour 30 minutes to complete the Unit 3 exam paper. The paper is worth 90 marks and there are three sections (Section A, B and C). The paper will contain multiple choice, short- and extended-answer, data response and scenario-based questions.

Using your knowledge of business assess   Multiple choice   Give, state and identify   Calculate

What is meant by the term

Question types   Outline   Describe

Assess   Discuss   Questions using diagrams   Choice questions   Explain

Context

When an exam question refers to a particular business, you need to answer the question in the CONTEXT of that business. This means that your answer must talk specifically about the business in the question.

To do this, you should think about:

☑ the products the business makes

☑ the industry in which it operates

☑ who the competitors are.

Understanding the question

Make sure that you read the questions and any other information carefully so you can understand what the question is asking you to do. Do you need to identify, explain, describe, discuss or assess something?

You should also look at the number of marks available and make sure you spend the appropriate amount of time on each question.

Worked example

target G-F

Amazon is a well known online retailer. It has grown by differentiating itself from its rivals and being highly competitive.

(a) Which **one** of the following elements of the marketing mix does this represent? Select **one** answer.   **(1 mark)**

A ☐ Price   C ☒ Promotion

B ☐ Product   D ☐ Place

target D-C

(b) Identify **two** methods Amazon might use to differentiate its service from its rivals.   **(2 marks)**

1   Lower prices

2   Convenience

target D-C

(c) Describe why developing a well known brand is important to the success of a business such as Amazon.   **(3 marks)**

Branding gives Amazon a clearer identity and personality. This will make Amazon stand out because the internet is very competitive.

There are three parts to this question and all three parts refer to Amazon. Make sure that you think about Amazon's products, business and competitors when answering the questions. There are three different question types here:

• Multiple choice   • Identify   • Describe

Make sure you understand what you need to do for each question.

Other possible answers include:

• improving quality   • more choice

• branding   • faster delivery.

You do not need to spend time writing lots of detail for 'give', 'state' and 'identify' questions.

EXAM ALERT!

More than one in ten students got all three marks for part **(c)**. You need to make three relevant points and refer specifically to **Amazon**.

This was a real exam question that a lot of students struggled with – **be prepared!**

Exam skills 2

In your exam you will have to answer six, eight and ten mark questions. These are called extended-writing questions. To answer an extended-writing question effectively you should:

- ✓ read the question and any other information carefully
- ✓ make sure you understand what the question is asking you to do – do you need to make a choice, discuss or assess something?
- ✓ use appropriate business concepts and terms
- ✓ develop your answer and support it with appropriate examples
- ✓ refer to the context given in the question (if there is one)
- ✓ make sure your answer is balanced.

Some of these questions are based around evidence and will give you a specific CONTEXT. You need to make sure that you apply your answer to the given context when answering these questions.

Worked example

 target
B-A

(a) Having a quality control system or a quality culture are two ways a business might try to improve quality. Which of these **two** do you think would be more successful in improving quality in a business and why?   **(6 marks)**

I think that a quality culture is more successful in improving quality because it includes all employees so is better for motivation. If employees feel included, they might be more satisfied as they are proud of doing a good job. It depends on the business culture though as it can take time to establish a quality culture...

target
A-A*

(b) Discuss the importance of increasing wages as a method of motivating workers employed in low-skilled industries.   **(6 marks)**

Increasing wages is an important motivator for low-skilled industries because low skill jobs are usually low paid. Also, these jobs might be more boring so money is important as there are few other motivators...

This is an extract from a student answer.

In this extract, the student has chosen 'quality culture' and has started to explain how this would be more successful in improving quality.

When answering this question you need **either** to refer to both quality control systems and quality culture, and evaluate why you have chosen the method **or** to focus solely on one method and provide analysis and balance around this method. Remember that there is no right answer to these questions but you need to make sure you justify your choice.

This is an extract from a student answer.

EXAM ALERT!

Only one in twenty students scored five or six marks for this question. You need to focus on the context and think about the **extent** to which money motivates a worker.

> This was a real exam question that a lot of students struggled with – **be prepared!**   ResultsPlus

In this extract the student has thought about the **context** of the question – workers in **low-skilled industries**. This means that their answer is focused appropriately on the reasons why money might motivate these workers in particular.

Exam skills 3

Some of the extended-writing questions in Sections B and C will be assessed for the quality of written communication (QWC). These questions are marked with an asterisk. When answering these questions you should make sure that:

- ✓ your answer is written to a high standard
- ✓ there are no errors in spelling, punctuation or grammar
- ✓ the quality of language is high
- ✓ your answer is clearly structured.

Worked example

This asterisk means that your answer will also be assessed for QWC.

target A–A*

* **(a)** Tesco has taken steps to reduce the effect of its operations on the environment. Assess **two** possible benefits to Tesco from doing this. **(8 marks)**

This is an extract from a student answer.

…How far these two things (adding value and premium pricing) will benefit Tesco depends on how important these benefits are to customers. Some customers might not care about the environment and only worry about the price of goods they buy from Tesco, so introducing premium pricing would actually be a drawback…

EXAM ALERT!

More than one in ten students scored four or more marks for this question. Your answer must contain **analysis** and **evaluation**. For example, you could consider the size and speed of any benefits, state which benefit is larger or more significant, or consider that benefits usually involve some kind of drawback.

This was a real exam question that a lot of students struggled with – **be prepared!**   ResultsPlus

target A–A*

* **(b)** Stuart Rose believes that a responsible business can be a profitable business. Using your knowledge of business, to what extent can a business like M&S be ethically responsible **and** profitable. Justify your answer. **(10 marks)**

This asterisk means that your answer will also be assessed for QWC.

This is an extract from a student answer.

…Overall, as M&S is a large firm that has economies of scale and the potential to reduce its production costs even further, it is possible to be ethically responsible and profitable to a large extent. However, the company needs to be careful about achieving the right balance because reducing production costs could damage quality or the company's reputation, which would then damage its profitability.

You must **justify** your answer. Your answer should have a clear, balanced argument for and against the possibility of absorbing higher costs, and include the appropriate business terminology, concepts and methods. You should finish with a well-supported conclusion.

Trade-offs

Scarcity and choice

The planet's resources are SCARCE. There is only a LIMITED amount of resources such as raw materials, fuel and time. But people usually have UNLIMITED needs or wants. For example, they might want:

- a bigger house or better car
- more meals out
- a better education or better healthcare
- a cleaner environment.

Because resources are scarce, people have to make CHOICES. They cannot have everything.

Trade-offs

Spending decisions often involve sacrifices or trade-offs. Jenny has £20 to spend and would like to buy four things.

By buying the make-up bag, Jenny has sacrificed the benefits from the other three items on the list. This is her TRADE-OFF.

> New make-up bag £20
>
> Two CDs £10 each
>
> Night out £20
>
> Charity donation £20

Worked example

Change4Life is a government project that encourages people to adopt a healthier lifestyle. Part of the project allows those aged under 18 and over 60 to swim for free in public swimming pools. Some people feel the opportunity cost of the £140 million spent on the project was too high. They believe the money could have been better spent on other things, such as education.

target C-B

Describe **two** possible trade-offs that the UK government might face in making a decision to fund projects such as Change4Life. **(4 marks)**

The government might sacrifice spending this money on health spending. People who are ill might not get treatment. The government might also cut education spending and not as many people could go to university.

Opportunity cost

OPPORTUNITY COST describes the benefit lost from the next best alternative when making a choice. So the opportunity cost to Jenny of buying the make-up bag is the benefit lost from not buying the CDs.

Other possible trade-offs include:
- spending on welfare benefits
- improvements to transport.

EXAM ALERT!

Four in ten students got all four marks for this question. You need to identify **two** trade-offs and describe them both.

This was a real exam question that a lot of students struggled with – **be prepared!**   ResultsPlus

---

Now try this

Colin Sankey runs a motor repair shop. He has £5000 to buy the resources below. They are listed in order of preference.

Priority	Resources	Cost
1	New van	£5000
2	Part-time office assistant	£5000
3	New hydraulic lift	£5000
4	Business advert on local radio	£5000

1. Outline **one** trade-off that Colin would have to make when choosing to purchase the new van. **(2 marks)**
target C-B

2. Use this example to define what is meant by opportunity cost. **(2 marks)**
target B-A

Raising and lowering prices

Businesses often change their prices to try and increase revenue. Some businesses benefit from cutting prices but others benefit from increasing prices.

Price and revenue

The PRICE is the amount of money consumers need to pay to buy a product.

REVENUE is the amount of money a business gets from selling its products in a period of time.

Revenue = Price x Quantity sold

Changing the price might increase or decrease revenues depending on how PRICE SENSITIVE demand for that product or service is.

Price sensitivity

Demand is INSENSITIVE to price changes if:
- ☑ there are few or no substitutes
- ☑ the product is essential / a necessity.

Demand is SENSITIVE to price changes if:
- ☑ there are many substitutes
- ☑ the product is a luxury item or not a necessity.

For most products, demand is PRICE SENSITIVE. This means that demand will change more when price changes. So increasing price will decrease demand, meaning that revenue could decrease.

| Price increase | Larger fall in demand | Decrease in revenue |
| Price decrease | Larger rise in demand | Increase in revenue |

If demand for a product is PRICE INSENSITIVE it means that demand will not change very much when price changes. So increasing the price will not impact on demand, meaning that revenue will increase.

| Price increase | Smaller fall in demand | Increase in revenue |
| Price decrease | Smaller rise in demand | Decrease in revenue |

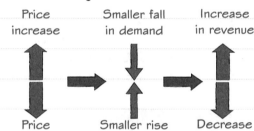

Worked example

One of the products targeted by the UK government for taxes is petrol.
What is the main reason for this?
Select **one** answer. **(1 mark)**

target D-C

A ☐ Demand for petrol is price sensitive
B ☐ Petrol is imported
C ☒ Demand for petrol is price insensitive
D ☐ The price of petrol has risen sharply in recent years

Make sure you think carefully about the specific product. The demand for petrol is price insensitive as there is no widely available substitute for it. Increasing price would not reduce demand very much and government revenue would increase.

Now try this

target A-A*

1 Consumers pick from a variety of chocolate bars, including *Mars Bars*, *Snickers*, *Dairy Milk* and *Double Decker*. Explain why the demand for one of these chocolate bars is likely to be price sensitive. **(3 marks)**

2 Explain how a business selling chocolate bars would benefit from a price decrease in one brand of chocolate bar. **(3 marks)**

Stakeholders

Different stakeholders often have different PERSPECTIVES and INTERESTS in a business. Their interests can be in conflict. You need to know about these conflicts and how some stakeholders can have more influence on decision-making than others.

Business stakeholders

Stakeholders are groups that have an interest in the performance of a business. Different stakeholders have different interests.

Stakeholder	Key interests
Shareholders	Profit, dividends and growth
Workers	Wages, job security and good conditions
Customers	Fair price, choice and good quality
Managers / directors	Pay, growth and power
Government	Competition and tax revenues
Local community	Jobs and clean environment

Stakeholder conflict

CONFLICTS are likely to occur between stakeholders if they have different interests.

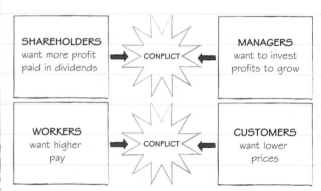

SHAREHOLDERS want more profit paid in dividends → CONFLICT ← MANAGERS want to invest profits to grow

WORKERS want higher pay → CONFLICT ← CUSTOMERS want lower prices

Stakeholder power

In some cases, certain stakeholder groups will be in a STRONGER POSITION than others and have more influence on decision-making. In 2010, workers in the private sector got pay increases of about 2%. However, executives saw their earnings rise by 55%. This suggests that managers had a powerful influence during the year.

Worked example

Change4Life is a government project that encourages people to adopt a healthier lifestyle. Part of the project allows those aged under 18 and over 60 to swim for free in public swimming pools.

target G-F

Identify **two** stakeholders that might benefit from the Change4Life project.   **(2 marks)**

1 Customers
2 Employees

Other examples of stakeholders for this project include government, local community and managers. You do not need to spend time writing a sentence when answering 'identify' questions – in this case one word is enough.

EXAM ALERT!

Six in ten students got both marks. In this question, you need to identify **two** stakeholders that might benefit from the Change4Life project, so the stakeholders need to be right for this context.

This was a real exam question that a lot of students struggled with – **be prepared!**

Results Plus

Now try this

Gerrard plc announced that it would abandon its plans to build a new chemical-processing plant near West Walton, Teesside. This followed a protest by local residents claiming that the effect on the local environment would be 'catastrophic'.

1 What is meant by the term 'stakeholder'?   **(2 marks)**

target F-E

2 Explain which group of stakeholders has the most influence on decision-making in this case.   **(3 marks)**

target E-D

Hidden costs or benefits

Economic decisions may have an impact on THIRD PARTIES (people or groups that have nothing to do with the decision). This means that stakeholders who have nothing to do with the decision are affected. These impacts are called EXTERNALITIES and may be positive or negative.

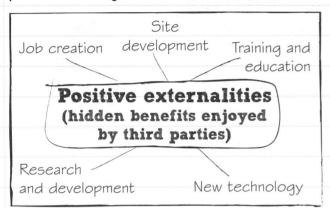

Job creation   Site development   Training and education

Positive externalities
(hidden benefits enjoyed by third parties)

Research and development   New technology

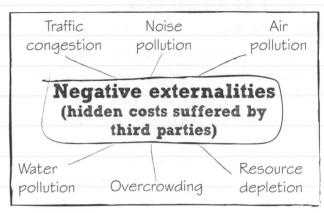

Traffic congestion   Noise pollution   Air pollution

Negative externalities
(hidden costs suffered by third parties)

Water pollution   Overcrowding   Resource depletion

Worked example

target
G–F

CleanUP plc is a waste-disposal firm that treats sewage. It intends to set up a new treatment plant on the edge of a village. The council and the residents can see both positive and negative externalities being created should the plant be built. The local council is considering approving the plans.

> Other examples of stakeholders might be customers of CleanUP, local suppliers, builders and banks.

(a) Identify **one** stakeholder that might be affected by the decision to allow CleanUP plc to build the treatment plant.   **(1 mark)**

Local residents

> The stakeholder effects must be linked directly to the nature of the externality and its effect.

target
E–D

(b) Explain how this stakeholder might be affected by the decision.   **(3 marks)**

Local residents would be affected by the decision to build the waste-disposal plant. Their normal environment would be disrupted. They may be troubled continually by the horrible smells coming from the plant. This may be extremely unpleasant and the value of their houses might fall.

Now try this

Morgan plc recently bought an abandoned plot of land in Hull containing run-down warehouses. It had become an eyesore and a danger to trespassers. On the site the company built a retail centre, a restaurant and flats for the elderly, costing £32 million. Morgan warned local residents that building would cause some disruption. The warehouse demolition created noise and dust. There was also 12 months of congestion due to the temporary closure of an important road.

target
C–B

1   Identify **two** negative externalities in this case.   **(2 marks)**

target
B–A

2   Explain **one** negative externality that Morgan plc might impose on local residents.   **(3 marks)**

> Externalities affect people or groups that have nothing to do with the decision.

Measuring success

Stakeholders interested in the financial success of a business are likely to look at PROFIT, REVENUE or MARKET SHARE. SOCIAL SUCCESS is also important. This is business performance in terms of social, environmental and ethical responsibility.

Profit and revenue

PROFIT is the:

- most common measure of success
- reward to the business owners
- reward for taking risk or showing enterprise
- difference between total costs and total revenue.

REVENUE is the money a business gets from selling its output. A growing market share or an increase in revenue is a sign of success.

Market share

MARKET SHARE is the quantity sold by a business as a percentage of the sales in a market. Tesco has the largest market share of UK supermarkets.

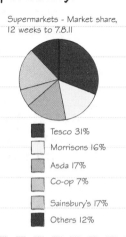

Supermarkets - Market share, 12 weeks to 7.8.11

- ■ Tesco 31%
- ☐ Morrisons 16%
- Asda 17%
- Co-op 7%
- Sainsbury's 17%
- ■ Others 12%

Social success

Some businesses produce a CORPORATE SOCIAL RESPONSIBILITY (CSR) report to measure its social success. It might look at:

- ✓ how well workers are treated
- ✓ levels of emissions and waste
- ✓ the use of recycled materials
- ✓ work-related accident rates
- ✓ the use of energy saving devices
- ✓ the firm's ethical stance.

Competitiveness and competitive advantage

COMPETITIVENESS is the strength of a firm's position in a market, measured by market share and profitability. It reflects whether consumers are prepared to use the business over its rivals.

COMPETITIVE ADVANTAGES are the advantages that firms have over their rivals. They help to win customers. These advantages need to be difficult to copy (defensible) and unique (distinctive).

Worked example

target D-C

Explain **one** way in which a business could measure its success.   **(3 marks)**

The most common way to measure success is by profit. If profit increases over time this would suggest that the business is improving its performance. Most owners would consider this to be successful.

> Other ways of measuring business success include revenue and profit margin.

Now try this

target C-B

1   Identify **three** possible sources of competitive advantage for a business.   **(3 marks)**

2   Explain how **one** of these sources might give a business a competitive advantage.   **(3 marks)**

> Do not confuse competitiveness with competitive advantage.

Causes of business failure

If a business does not have enough money to pay its bills over a prolonged period of time it is said to be INSOLVENT. This usually results in BUSINESS FAILURE. There are a number of reasons why this might happen.

Marketing mix

To survive, businesses have to be competitive. They must meet consumers' needs better than their rivals do. They may lose competitiveness if they get part of the MARKETING MIX wrong.

Errors in the marketing mix:

- ⊗ Price – too low or too high.
- ⊗ Product – poor quality or doesn't meet customer needs.
- ⊗ Promotion – wrong media or wrongly targeted.
- ⊗ Place – poor delivery record or not available online.

Productivity

PRODUCTIVITY is the output per worker or machine over a period of time. If productivity falls, business costs may rise. Poor productivity may be caused by:

- inadequate training or demotivated workers
- bad management
- out-of-date machinery
- a lack of flexibility.

The importance of cash flow

Businesses need to make sure that they have enough cash when they need it. Without cash a business cannot trade – it will fail. CASH FLOW problems may be caused by:

- an unexpected fall in demand
- allowing too much trade credit
- seasonal demand
- poor cash management
- unexpected expenditure or bad debts.

Changing market conditions and competition

Some businesses fail because demand for their products falls. Why might this happen?

- A fall in income – perhaps due to a recession.
- A change in tastes or fashion – new trends can change demand.
- Advertising – a lack of advertising or poor adverts can change demand.
- Increased competition – new rivals with better products will affect demand.

Worked example

target **G-F**

In 2011, many retailers such as Oddbins, Habitat and Focus DIY failed, mainly because of the recession. Explain how a recession causes a change in demand for the products of these retailers. **(3 marks)**

A recession usually leads to a fall in demand. People may lose their jobs and have less income. As their income is lower, they are less likely to buy wine, furniture or housing materials such as those sold by Oddbins, Habitat and Focus DIY.

You need to make three clearly linked statements to 'explain how a recession causes a change in demand'.

Now try this

target **C-B**

1. Which of the following is most likely to lead to a fall in productivity? Select **one** answer. **(1 mark)**

   A ☐ An increase in price

   B ☐ A decrease in price

   C ☐ Installing new technology

   D ☐ A decline in worker motivation

Problems faced by the economy 1

A major problem that an economy might face is rising prices. This is called INFLATION. You need to know the causes and effects of inflation. You also need to know what is meant by the level of DEMAND, what causes it to change, and how this can affect businesses.

The level of demand in the economy

The LEVEL OF DEMAND refers to spending that takes place in an economy. Demand can come from CONSUMERS, GOVERNMENT, BUSINESSES or FOREIGNERS.

You need to know how the level of demand can affect businesses.

Demand rises → Business sales may benefit → Risk may be reduced

Demand falls → Business sales may suffer → Risk may increase

What might change demand?

Demand in the economy may go up or down because of:

- THE LEVEL OF ECONOMIC ACTIVITY – if there is a recession, demand will fall.
- INTEREST RATES – if interest rates fall, borrowing and demand will increase.
- CONSUMER CONFIDENCE – if consumers think their jobs might be lost, they might cut their spending.
- FOREIGN DEMAND – if the pound gets weaker, foreign demand will rise.

Inflation and its effects

INFLATION is the change in the average level of prices in the economy. It is measured using the consumer price index (CPI). It measures changes in the price of food, housing, clothing and other products. Inflation may harm individuals and the economy. There may be:

- an increase in the cost of living and lower living standards
- a fall in business profits
- an increase in uncertainty
- a fall in confidence.

What causes inflation?

You need to know the main causes of inflation.

- **Rising demand.** If demand rises faster than supply, prices may rise. This could be caused by lower interest rates, rising wages or improved consumer confidence.
- **Rising costs.** If the cost of wages, ingredients, materials, utilities or any other business expense goes up, firms may raise prices to protect profit.

Worked example

target B-A

Explain **one** effect of inflation on a business.   **(3 marks)**

A rise in raw material prices can cause a firm's costs to rise. Rising costs of production will reduce the firm's profits. This may result in the firm increasing its prices to remain profitable.

There must be a clear explanation of how a rise in inflation can affect a business, using links between points. In this answer the student has explained how costs, profits and prices are affected.

Now try this

1 Explain how rising costs might cause inflation.

target B-A   **(3 marks)**

2 Explain how a fall in consumer confidence might affect the demand for clothes.   **(3 marks)**

target C-B

Problems faced by the economy 2

Unemployment is a problem for the economy. You need to know about the costs of unemployment to individuals and society. You also need to know the effects that INTERNAL and EXTERNAL SHOCKS can have on the economy.

What is unemployment?

UNEMPLOYMENT exists when people who want to find work cannot do so.

Unemployment can be measured by counting the number of people who claim unemployment benefits or the number of people in a survey who say they are looking for work.

Effects of unemployment

To individuals	To society
Lower incomes	Less tax revenue / spending
Falling living standards	Need to cut prices
Loss of self-esteem	Higher benefits
Stress or depression	Lower output
Family tensions	Increased crime
Difficulties such as divorce	Less social interaction
Loss of skills	Decline in standards of behaviour
Health problems	Less enterprise

External shocks

The economy can be affected by events that are beyond the control of the government. They normally damage the economy and are called EXTERNAL SHOCKS. Examples are:

- a rise in the price of a key commodity such as oil
- a world political event such as a war
- an international disaster
- a global recession
- changes in exchange rates.

Internal shocks

INTERNAL SHOCKS can also damage the economy. They are unexpected changes in demand caused by events within a country.

A national banking crisis

Freak local weather conditions

Examples of internal shocks

A national strike

A rapid rise in domestic property prices

Worked example

target
D-C

Which of the following is most likely to be an example of an external shock to the UK economy? Select **one** answer.   **(1 mark)**

A ☐ A rise in domestic interest rates

B ☐ A rise in the UK rate of inflation

C ☐ A national strike

D ☒ A fall in the price of oil

The price of oil is determined on an international market. All of the other options are examples of **internal shocks**.

Now try this

target
C-B

target
D-C

1 Define the term 'unemployment'.   **(2 marks)**

2 Explain **one** way in which society might be affected by high levels of unemployment. **(3 marks)**

Exchange rates 1

Different countries use different currencies. When trading, it is necessary to calculate how much one currency is worth in terms of the other. This is called the EXCHANGE RATE. You need to understand how exchange rates can change.

International trade

Countries such as the UK exchange goods and services. The exchange of products between different countries is called INTERNATIONAL TRADE.

What is an exchange rate?

The exchange rate is the value of one currency in terms of another, so £1 = €1.20, £1 = US$1.58, or £1 = ¥122. Exchange rates can affect trade.

EXAMPLE: A UK business buys $200000 of goods from a US supplier. How much will this cost in pounds if £1 = $1.58?

ANSWER: $200000 ÷ $1.58 = £126582

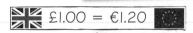 £1.00 = €1.20

If the pound increases in value against other currencies it is said to STRENGTHEN. The pound can buy more euros, or fewer pounds are needed to buy one euro.

£1.00 = €1.10

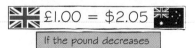 £1.00 = $2.05

If the pound decreases in value against other currencies it is said to WEAKEN. The pound buys fewer Australian dollars, or more pounds are needed to buy one Australian dollar.

£1.00 = $1.46

What causes the exchange rate to change?

Exchange rates change all the time. They are determined by MARKET FORCES. Exchange rates are affected by:

- the demand for imports
- the demand for exports
- interest rates.

Worked example

 target **D-C**

Define the term 'international trade'.

(2 marks)

International trade is when countries import and export goods and services from and to each other.

EXAM ALERT!

Half of students got full marks for this answer. You need to mention both imports and exports. You could include a clear example in your answer.

 This was a real exam question that a lot of students struggled with – **be prepared!** Results**Plus**

Now try this

target **B-A**

1 State **two** factors that might cause the value of the exchange rate to change.   **(2 marks)**

2 The value of the pound changes from £1 = $2 to £1 = $1.60. Explain whether it has weakened or strengthened.   **(3 marks)**

 target **C-B**

Exchange rates 2

Changes in the exchange rate can affect businesses in different ways because they affect the PRICE of imports and exports. You need to know how businesses are affected by exchange rate changes.

1 The effect on a UK EXPORTER of a STRENGTHENING in the exchange rate

> POUND GETS STRONGER
>
> PRICE OF EXPORTS RISES
>
> DEMAND FOR EXPORTS FALLS
>
> REVENUE AND PROFITS FALL

2 The effect on a UK IMPORTER of a STRENGTHENING in the exchange rate

> POUND GETS STRONGER
>
> PRICE OF IMPORTS FALL
>
> COSTS FALL
>
> PROFITS RISE

3 The effect on a UK EXPORTER of a WEAKENING in the exchange rate

> POUND GETS WEAKER
>
> PRICE OF EXPORTS FALLS
>
> DEMAND FOR EXPORTS RISES
>
> REVENUE AND PROFITS RISES

4 The effect on a UK IMPORTER of a WEAKENING in the exchange rate

> POUND GETS WEAKER
>
> PRICE OF IMPORTS RISE
>
> COSTS RISE
>
> PROFITS FALL

Worked example

target B-A

Assess the effect of a weakening pound against the euro on the profits of high-street retailers. **(8 marks)**

...High-street retailers have to buy in stock from abroad and this might increase in price. If the retailer passes this price rise to consumers to protect profit, this could lead to a decrease in sales. This depends on the price sensitivity of the products because...

This is an extract from a student answer.

EXAM ALERT!

One in three students scored between six and eight marks for this question. You need to refer to one or more effects and give at least **two** reasons, provide balance in your answer and refer to high-street retailers.

This was a real exam question that a lot of students struggled with – **be prepared!**

ResultsPlus

Now try this

target D-C

1 If £1 = $2, how much would a UK importer pay for $400 000 of goods?
Select **one** answer. **(1 mark)**

A ☐ $400 000   B ☐ £400 000   C ☐ £200 000   D ☐ £800 000

target C-B

2 If the pound weakens, which of the following is most likely to occur?
Select **one** answer. **(1 mark)**

A ☐ International trade will cease   C ☐ The price of imports will fall

B ☐ The price of imports will rise   D ☐ The price of exports will rise

The government 1

The government is responsible for managing the ECONOMY and responding to SOCIAL ISSUES such as health, education, crime and poverty. You need to know what tools the government has to do this.

Government policy tools

The government has tools that it uses to influence the level of ECONOMIC ACTIVITY (the amount of buying and selling that takes place in the economy):

- MONETARY POLICY – using changes in interest rates to influence economic activity.
- FISCAL POLICY – using taxation and government spending to achieve government objectives.

Interest rates

The INTEREST RATE:

- is the price paid to borrow money
- is a reward to savers
- affects purchases of consumer durables and housing
- affects business purchases of machinery, tools and equipment
- is set by the Bank of England.

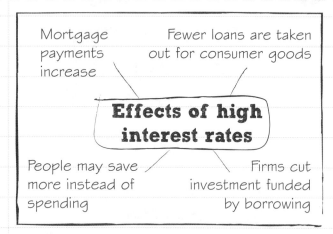

Mortgage payments increase

Fewer loans are taken out for consumer goods

Effects of high interest rates

People may save more instead of spending

Firms cut investment funded by borrowing

Taxation and government spending

TAXATION is used to:

- raise revenue to fund government spending
- regulate demand in the economy
- change behaviour.

GOVERNMENT SPENDING is used to:

- provide essential public services
- regulate demand in the economy
- resolve social issues, such as child poverty.

Worked example

target
C-B

Explain **one** way in which higher interest rates reduce demand in the economy. **(3 marks)**

When interest rates rise, the cost of borrowing increases. This means that payments charging interest, such as mortgage repayments, increase and people have less disposable income. Consequently their demand for certain goods and services, such as non-essentials, will fall.

You need to make three clearly linked statements to 'explain one way in which higher interest rates reduce demand in the economy'.

Golden tip

HIGH interest rates REDUCE demand.
LOW interest rates INCREASE demand.

Now try this

target
C-B

target
E-D

1 Define the term 'interest rate'. **(2 marks)**

2 State **three** reasons why the government imposes taxes. **(3 marks)**

The government 2

The government tries to deal with inflation and unemployment using fiscal policy and monetary policy. It also uses fiscal policy to try to resolve social problems.

Reducing inflation

Monetary policy

Higher interest rates should reduce the demand for loans, as people would have more to pay back. With fewer loans, demand in the economy will fall, leading to less pressure on prices.

Fiscal policy

To relieve pressure on prices, the government could reduce demand by cutting its own spending and / or raising taxes. Higher income taxes will reduce consumer demand.

Reducing unemployment

More demand in the economy helps to create jobs. Businesses have to produce more to meet increased demand, and to produce more they will need more workers. The government can increase demand by:

- lowering interest rates
- lowering taxes
- increasing government expenditure.

Fiscal policy and social issues

Examples of government fiscal policy include:

- benefits given to poor families to help avoid child poverty
- payments to pensioners during the winter to meet heating costs
- taxes on cigarettes to discourage smoking
- taxes on drivers in central London to avoid congestion
- taxes on alcohol to discourage binge drinking.

How effective are taxes at changing habits?

Taxes designed to change habits may or may not work.

Congestion still exists in London, on motorways and in other urban areas.

The number of smokers has fallen in recent years.

Worked example

target
D–C

Which **one** of the following measures is **most likely** to reduce unemployment? **(1 mark)**

A ☐ An increase in corporation tax

B ☐ Lower interest rates

C ☒ Higher interest rates

B ☐ Cuts in government expenditure

Lowering interest rates creates more demand in the economy, so businesses have to produce more to meet demand. This leads to a reduction in unemployment.

Now try this

target
E–D

1 (a) Identify **one** method that the government could use to reduce binge drinking. **(1 mark)**

   (b) Explain how this method might lead to a reduction in binge drinking. **(3 marks)**

target
D–C

How businesses grow

Once a business is established and successful, most owners want it to grow. There are different approaches to growth and you need to understand the difference between them.

Internal growth

A business grows when it sells more output over a period of time. BUSINESS GROWTH is often an important objective because it may:

- help to increase market share
- lead to lower costs
- result in more profit.

INTERNAL GROWTH is when a firm increases its size by selling more of its output without the involvement of other businesses.

Methods of internal growth

- Changing the marketing mix – for example, finding new markets.
- Innovation – the successful commercial exploitation of an invention.
- Research and development – developing a new product which is not currently available.

External growth

A faster way for a business to grow is for it to join forces with another. There are two approaches to EXTERNAL GROWTH.

- MERGER – where two or more firms agree to join up. This is a voluntary agreement with both firms retaining their identities.
- TAKEOVER – where one business buys another. To take over a company it is necessary to gain control by buying enough shares.

Methods of external growth

Mergers and takeovers can take place when firms join at different stages of production.

Backward vertical – firm joins with one at a previous stage (e.g. a supplier)

Conglomerate – firms with no common business interest join

Horizontal – firms at the same stage join

Forward vertical – firm joins with one at a later stage (e.g. a customer)

Worked example

Identify **two** reasons why a business might want to grow. **(2 marks)**

1 Higher profit
2 Economies of scale

Other possible answers include to get a bigger market share, or to dominate the market.

Remember that you do not need to write lots in 'identify' questions – this student achieved two marks for identifying **two** reasons.

Now try this

target E-D

1 Which of the following is a definition of the term 'merger'? Select **one** answer. **(1 mark)**

A merger is where:

A ☐ two or more businesses voluntarily join together

B ☐ one business buys enough shares in another business to control it

C ☐ two businesses work together to design a new product

D ☐ one business takes over another company

target C-B

2 Describe the difference between internal and external growth. **(4 marks)**

Why businesses grow

You need to understand both the advantages and disadvantages of growth.

Reasons for growth

- **Survival** – big firms can reinvest profits to improve and to fight off takeover bids.
- **Higher returns** – more revenue and bigger profits for the owners.
- **Lower costs** – firms can exploit economies of scale as they grow.
- **Market power** – big firms can dominate the market and pressurise suppliers.
- **Spread risk** – big firms can develop new products and break into new markets.

Drawbacks to growth

INFLEXIBILITY – big firms might struggle or take too long to adapt to change.

HIGHER COSTS – firms that get too big might suffer from diseconomies of scale.

LOSS OF FOCUS – giant firms might make a bad decision, which can be very expensive.

Economies of scale

As firms grow their average costs fall. This is because they receive discounts for buying larger amounts of resources, and they use larger and more efficient machinery, which lowers costs.

44.5p / pint MILK 2 PINTS 89p   29.5p / pint MILK 4 PINTS £1.18   29p / pint MILK 6 PINTS £1.74

Diseconomies of scale

If a firm gets too big, its average costs may rise. Reasons for this can include:

- poor co-ordination – it is more difficult to manage a firm with 70000 employees than one with 7 employees
- poor communication – it may be harder to communicate with teams and departments that are scattered across the globe.

Worked example

target B-A

Describe **one** possible disadvantage for a business when it grows in size.   **(4 marks)**

When a business grows it might face diseconomies of scale. The average costs may rise as it becomes too big it cannot compete. The increased costs of purchasing new machinery may not bring increased output and sales and may force an increase in prices.

EXAM ALERT!

Fewer than three in twenty students got all four marks for this answer. Make sure you describe the disadvantage – such as diseconomies of scale – by including the implications for costs, prices and profits in your answer.

This was a real exam question that a lot of students struggled with – **be prepared!**   ResultsPlus

Now try this

target A-A*

1   Explain **one** way in which a business might benefit from economies of scale.   **(3 marks)**

Monopoly power

Many would argue that consumers will be exploited when a MONOPOLY dominates the market. However, you also need to be aware that, sometimes, consumers can benefit from a monopoly.

What is a monopoly?

- A MONOPOLIST is a firm that supplies a large part of the market.
- MONOPOLY POWER means having some control or influence over the market.
- A PURE monopolist is able to control 100% of a market.
- The government says a monopoly exists when a firm controls at least 25% of the market.
- LOCAL monopolies can exist, for example if there is only one pub or shop in a village.
- NATURAL monopolies are where costs are lower if one large business supplies the market.

Monopoly – good or bad?

GOOD		BAD
Value for money because they can lower costs by exploiting economies of scale		**Higher prices** due to a lack of competition in the market
New product development because monopolies have more resources and can get patents	OR	**Restricted choice** that denies people of variety in their lives
Natural monopolies reduce waste because they avoid duplication		**Restricted entry** that makes it difficult for new rivals to get into the market
Higher returns for shareholders		**Excessive profits** due to their power and dominance

Worked example

target **C-B**

Explain **one** disadvantage of a monopoly to consumers. **(3 marks)**

A monopoly is able to increase the price that consumers pay because there is limited competition. This means customers would have no choice but to use the monopoly, whatever price it charges, so may be worse off.

EXAM ALERT!

Four in ten students scored three marks for this question. You need to make sure you develop your answer to clearly explain why the point you have identified is a disadvantage of a monopoly to consumers.

This was a real exam question that a lot of students struggled with – **be prepared!** ResultsPlus

Other disadvantages of monopolies include:
- restricting new entrants to the market
- less choice for consumers.

Now try this

target **B-A**

1 Define the term 'monopoly'. One single supplier by supplying goods and services, 25% market share. **(2 marks)**

target **D-C**

2 State **two** possible benefits to society of monopolies. **(2 marks)**

Development of products increase due to monopoly having more resources
Better value for money as they can lower costs

Controlling big businesses

Many would argue that big businesses should be controlled because they may be in a position to exploit consumers. You need to understand that there are different approaches to such control.

The role of authorities

REGULATORY BODIES or COMPETITION AUTHORITIES try to ensure that:

- fair competition exists in markets
- businesses act in the public interest
- firms avoid anti-competitive behaviour
- prices are not too high
- the quality of goods are up to standard.

Competition authorities

- The Competition Commission (CC) investigates markets for anti-competitive behaviour.
- The Office of Fair Trading enforces trading laws and conducts market studies.
- Specialist regulators regulate one specific industry (e.g. Ofwat regulates water and sewerage providers).
- The EU Competition Commission is similar to the CC, but covers all the EU.

Self regulation

SELF-REGULATION is where an industry monitors its own actions, to ensure that they are in the public interest. A code of conduct may be drawn up. This is a list of guidelines and good practice. Critics argue that self-regulation can't work because there is too much self-interest. Supporters say it will work because there is always the fear of government intervention.

Pressure groups

Pressure groups aim to influence the decisions of business, government and individuals

⬇

They unite people so that they have more power acting as one group

⬇

They use tactics such as boycotts, protests, marches and advertising to raise their profiles

⬇

Their success depends on whether they can gain public support and how much money they have

Worked example

target **A–A***

Describe the role of the Competition Commission in controlling businesses with monopoly power. **(4 marks)**

The Competition Commission (CC) can investigate markets where firms are engaging in anti-competitive behaviour, such as price-fixing. It cannot investigate itself, but responds to public complaints or follows instructions from the Office of Fair Trading. It can take action, such as blocking a merger, if it thinks that firms' behaviour is not in the public interest.

Make sure you:
- clearly explain the role of the Competition Commission
- show clear use of key terms and accurate descriptions.

Now try this

target **C–B**

1 Define the term 'pressure group'. *An organisation which aims to influence the decision of businesses or governments.* **(2 marks)**

2 A business is exploiting its customers by charging high prices. Explain why pressure-group tactics might cause a business to change its actions. **(3 marks)**

Pressure groups would advertise the problem to unite the public. They could do this using protests to influence the businesses decision.

Growth

If more output is produced, the economy has grown. You need to know how GROWTH is measured, what causes growth and what the government can do to help the economy grow.

What is economic growth?

Over time, economies tend to grow. This means that the amount of goods and services produced in the economy will increase. Generally, ECONOMIC GROWTH means that most people will be better off.

> Remember that economic growth can be negative. This means that the amount produced in the economy can actually fall.

- Economic growth is measured by adding up the value of all goods and services produced in the economy in one year.
- This total is called the GROSS DOMESTIC PRODUCT (GDP).
- The ANNUAL PERCENTAGE CHANGE in GDP is used to record growth.
- The average growth rate in the UK is usually between 2% and 3%, but in recent years it has been lower and sometimes negative owing to a recession.

What causes growth?

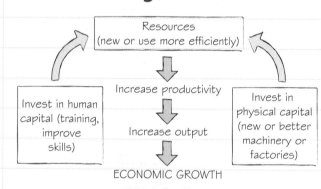

Resources (new or use more efficiently)

Invest in human capital (training, improve skills)

Increase productivity

Increase output

ECONOMIC GROWTH

Invest in physical capital (new or better machinery or factories)

What can the government do?

- Encourage investment in physical capital by lowering interest rates, offering grants or lowering tax on investment.
- Invest in the infrastructure by improving transport links.
- Improve the quality of human capital by investing in education.
- Encourage more consumption by lowering interest rates or lowering personal taxes.

Worked example

target A-A*

Two methods of stimulating economic growth include reductions in interest rates and taxation.

In your opinion, which of these **two** methods is more likely to increase economic growth and why? **(8 marks)**

> Make sure you refer to the method(s), develop your points, use appropriate business concepts and refer to the context of the question.

Cutting taxation is the better option as it benefits all consumers as reductions in VAT help those consumers who do not pay income tax. Reductions in interest rates however do not benefit those who do not have a mortgage and actually disadvantage people such as pensioners who are on fixed incomes...

> This is an extract from a student answer.

Now try this

target F-E

target C-B

1. Which of the following is used to measure economic growth? **(1 mark)**

   A ☐ Consumer prices index   B ☐ Value of imports   C ☐ Economies of scale   D ☐ GDP

2. Explain how investment in machinery can help the economy to grow. **(3 marks)**

Growth and standard of living

The STANDARD OF LIVING refers to the amount of goods and services a person can buy with their income in a year. If a person has more income, they can buy more goods and their living standard has risen. Standard of living is measured in GDP PER CAPITA (i.e. GDP ÷ population). This shows the AVERAGE living standard of a country and can be used to make comparisons.

The problems of using GDP

GDP per capita is not always a reliable measure of living standards because:

- if the population is small, GDP rates can give an inaccurate picture
- GDP is an average and assumes that everyone earns the same, but some earn a lot less and some a lot more
- GDP may be understated because some output may not be counted.

What other indicators measure living standards?

- INFANT MORTATLITY RATES – the percentage of babies that do not survive past their fifth birthday.
- LIFE EXPECTANCY RATES – the average age that people are expected to live to from birth.
- LITERACY RATES – the percentage of adults who are able to read and write.

Quality of life

The QUALITY OF LIFE is an individual's overall well-being. Here are some factors that can influence it.

Levels of education

People's health

The spare time people have

Number and quality of friends

Quality of family relationships

Worked example

target D-C

Explain how economic growth might improve the standard of living of a country.   **(3 marks)**

Economic growth results in more output being produced, which causes prices to fall. People can now purchase more goods and services with their income.

You need to clearly explain how economic growth improves the standard of living, making clear use of links and terminology.

Now try this

target C-B

1 Define the term 'standard of living'.
   (2 marks)

target B-A

2 Explain **one** problem with using GDP per capita as a measure of living standards.   **(3 marks)**

Can growth be bad?

Although economic growth can help raise people's living standards, you need to understand that it can also be bad. For example, many argue that economic growth can damage the environment.

The drawbacks of growth

- NEGATIVE EXTERNALITIES. There may be undesirable effects on third parties, as shown in the diagram.
- STRESS AND HEALTH PROBLEMS. Workers may be put under pressure to work harder, to become more efficient and to increase productivity. Overworked people may become stressed or ill.
- RISE IN PRICES. A growth in demand for commodities can lead to price increases.

Congestion
Higher incomes have increased car ownership.

Resource depletion
Non-renewable resources can never be replaced.

Negative externalities

Waste
Disposing of extra waste, e.g. packaging, increases costs.

Pollution
Air, water and noise pollution from more business activity.

Worked example

Pollution and the use of non-renewable resources are two drawbacks of economic growth. Which of these do you think is more serious and why? **(6 marks)**

Economic growth involves using up more resources, some of which, such as oil, cannot be replaced. Increased business activity can also cause pollution. Of these two drawbacks I think resource depletion is the more serious because…

- This question requires **evaluation**, which means you need to make a **judgement**.
- You have to decide which negative externality is more serious and **justify** your decision.
- You might consider the effects on future generations, or you could take an 'it depends' approach – for example, it depends whether there is a renewable resource that can replace the non-renewable resources.

This is an extract from a student answer.

Remember, there is no right or wrong answer to this question. The quality of the evaluation and analysis is the key to a good answer.

Now try this

1   (a) State **three** negative effects associated with growth. **(3 marks)**

   (b) Explain how **one** of these effects can be a problem for society. **(3 marks)**

Sustainable growth

If GDP can be increased without imposing negative externalities on future generations, economic growth is said to be sustainable. SUSTAINABLE GROWTH involves using more renewable resources.

The benefits of using renewable resources

To businesses

- Lower costs, e.g. by using cheaper recycled materials.
- Improved image, because they are seen to be more socially responsible.

To the wider economy

- Less pollution, e.g. by using wind power instead of coal to generate electricity.
- Future generations will have more non-renewable resources to use.

The drawbacks of using renewable resources

To businesses

- High set-up costs, e.g. expensive plant may be needed to use renewable or recycled resources.

To the wider economy

- Higher costs, e.g. using renewable energy to generate electricity is dearer.
- Other environmental problems may arise, e.g. unsightly wind farms.

How can business behave more responsibly?

Many firms try to be good corporate citizens. This means they try to be socially responsible. They may do this by:

- meeting the needs of a wider group of stakeholders
- adopting ethical codes of practice, such as refusing to deal with firms that sell guns
- carrying out CORPORATE SOCIAL RESPONSIBILITY audits, where firms assess their impact on society and the environment
- using renewable resources.

Why might businesses behave more responsibly?

- To avoid breaking the law.
- In response to media or public pressure.
- To attract ethical investors.
- To improve their image and raise sales.

Some businesses try to appear environmentally friendly in advertising even though they are actually not. This is called GREENWASH.

Worked example

target B-A

Explain **one** benefit to the wider economy of businesses being required to use more renewable resources. **(3 marks)**

Using renewable resources will benefit future generations because they can be used over and over again. It also means that there will be more non-renewable resources left for future generations.

You need to identify a key benefit and give reasons why it is a benefit. You do not need to spend time defining renewable resources in this question.

Now try this

target D-C

1   Define the term 'sustainable growth'.
(2 marks)

target C-B

2   State **two** ways in which a business could behave more responsibly.   **(2 marks)**

Government action

The government can take a number of measures to protect the environment. These measures are aimed at changing human behaviour.

Taxes and subsidies

TAXATION can affect people's behaviour.

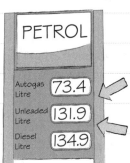

SUBSIDIES might be given to consumers or businesses for certain goods, Liquid Petroleum Gas (LPG) is taxed less heavily by the government because it is greener than petrol or diesel.

PETROL

Autogas Litre **73.4**
Unleaded Litre **131.9**
Diesel Litre **134.9**

Vehicle Excise Duty (VED) is higher on cars which use more petrol, or produce higher emissions.

Legislation

The UK and the EU have passed laws to protect the environment and prevent pollution.

- AIR LEGISLATION controls emissions, dark smoke and other airborne pollutants.
- WATER LEGISLATION aims to control water quality and conserve water resources.
- WASTE LEGISLATION controls the disposal, generation and transportation of waste.

Penalties for breaking the law include fines and imprisonment.

Regulation

REGULATION is a 'softer' approach to controlling businesses, using rules, guidelines and codes of practice to minimise pollution. For example, in agriculture there is a code of practice for the handling and storage of fertiliser. This is designed to reduce water pollution.

The effect of government measures on business

Measures aimed at protecting the environment can raise business costs. For example, firms may need to train staff, adapt work practices or buy new machinery. They might react by:

- some firms raising prices or increasing efficiency
- differentiating their products by suggesting that they are environmentally friendly.

Some firms may benefit from government measures – e.g. subsidies on electric vans make them cheaper, so demand will rise.

Worked example

target **E-D**

Which of the following measures is **most likely** to reduce pollution?   **(1 mark)**

A ☐ Relaxing guidelines on construction sites

B ☐ A subsidy to farmers using powerful nitrates

C ☒ Legislation to minimise industrial discharges into UK waterways

D ☐ Lower fines for waste disposal

A law to minimise industrial discharges into UK waterways should reduce water pollution. Discharges by firms are a major cause of water pollution. The other answers are likely to lead to greater pollution.

Now try this

target **D-C**

1 State **two** ways in which a business might react to government measures designed to reduce pollution.

    (2 marks)

target **A-A***

2 Economic growth can lead to problems such as pollution. Using your knowledge of business and economics, assess the case for governments using regulation as the best way to achieve sustainable growth.   **(10 marks)**

Is everybody equal?

All over the world there are huge inequalities of wealth and income. Some people are millionaires while, at the same time, many others rely on state benefits.

What is poverty?

There is no single definition of poverty.

- ABSOLUTE POVERTY is when people are unable to afford the basics of life such as food, shelter and clothes.
- RELATIVE POVERTY is when people can't afford the goods and services, including some luxuries, that are considered 'normal' in that country.
- THE POVERTY LINE is the extent to which people in a country live in poverty, e.g. the number of families living on less than a certain amount per week.

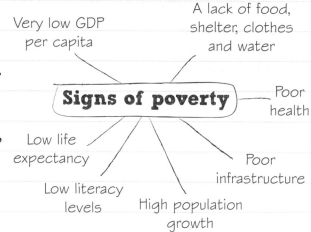

Signs of poverty
- Very low GDP per capita
- A lack of food, shelter, clothes and water
- Poor health
- Poor infrastructure
- High population growth
- Low literacy levels
- Low life expectancy

How can poverty be reduced?

In some countries, the WELFARE STATE has eliminated absolute poverty and reduced income inequalities by providing benefits and services funded from taxation.

- Child Benefits are paid to parents for each child they have under the age of 16.
- Working Tax Credits are paid to families on low incomes, depending on what they earn (they are means tested).
- There is free health care and free primary and secondary education available.

Standard of living

Data from different SOURCES can be used to judge a person's living standards. A person in Burundi is likely to have a LOWER standard of living than one in France, as the country has more people below the poverty line, and a lower life expectancy, literacy rate and GDP per head.

2011	France	Burundi
GDP per capita (US$)	35000	400
Population below poverty line	6%	68%
Life expectancy	81 yrs	59 yrs
Literacy rate	99%	59%

Worked example

target
G-F

Which of the following best describes the meaning of relative poverty?   **(1 mark)**

It is where people:

A ☒ are unable to afford many luxuries

B ☐ have no money

C ☐ are unable to afford the basics of life

D ☐ have to claim state benefits

> Relative poverty is when people can't afford the goods and services, including some luxuries that are considered 'normal' in that country.

Now try this

target
E-D

1   State **three** signs of absolute poverty in a country.   **(3 marks)**

target
D-C

2   Explain **one** method a government could use to reduce relative poverty.   **(3 marks)**

International trade 1

INTERNATIONAL TRADE is the exchange of goods and services between countries. You need to understand that trade can help less economically developed countries (LEDCs) to develop, although there are some drawbacks.

Benefits of international trade

More consumer choice

Living standards are raised, leading to higher levels of output and income

LEDCs can specialise in the production of goods in which they are efficient

Nations can obtain goods that cannot be produced domestically

Nations can obtain goods that others can produce more cheaply

LEDCs are provided with income, which they can spend on goods they can't produce or invest in education and infrastructure

Enables resource-rich countries to sell their products to foreign markets

Trade costs to LEDCs

The problems with trade for LEDCs are the threat to domestic producers from cheap imports and overspecialisation. Examples of costs may be:

- increased foreign competition, which drives down prices
- higher unemployment
- lower tax receipts for the government
- the loss of important industries in the long term.

The single European market

The SINGLE EUROPEAN MARKET is an example of a TRADING UNION. All trading restrictions have been removed between member countries in the European Union (EU). This has helped to raise living standards for members by:

- providing more choice and faster growth
- exploiting economies of scale
- encouraging more cooperation and foreign investment.

Worked example

 target **C-B**

Explain **one** cost to a less economically developed country (LEDC) of international trade.   **(3 marks)**

International trade creates increased foreign competition. This drives down prices in the LEDC as consumers can find cheaper products from abroad. This means that GDP will be lower in the LEDC than in a richer country.

EXAM ALERT!

Fewer than three in ten students got three marks for this question. In this answer the cost identified is 'competition', one consequence is 'drives down prices' and a second consequence is 'GDP will be lower'.

This was a real exam question that a lot of students struggled with – **be prepared!**   Results Plus

Now try this

target **D-C**

1   Define the term 'international trade'.   **(2 marks)**

 target **A-A***

2   Explain **one** way that the single European market might have led to improvements in living standards within the EU.   **(3 marks)**

International trade 2

Although FREE TRADE (where products are exchanged without restrictions) can help to raise living standards, some countries take measures to restrict trade. You need to understand the measures used and the reasons for such actions.

The restriction of trade is called PROTECTIONISM. Various methods can be used to restrict trade.

Tariffs
Taxes on imports

Quotas
Physical limits on imports

Trade restrictions

Non-tariff barriers
Imposing quality or safety standards

Subsidies
Money given to help domestic producers

Reasons for trade barriers

- Protecting jobs in domestic industries.
- Protecting infant industries.
- Preventing the dumping of cheap goods on the domestic market and the entry of undesirable goods.
- Raising revenue from tariffs.

Benefits and drawbacks of multinational corporations to LEDCs

A MULTINATIONAL CORPORATION (MNC) is a large company with operating facilities and markets around the world.

👍 Tax revenues for the government
👍 Employment opportunities
👍 An increase in GDP per capita for locals
👍 Increase in exports
👍 Development of infrastructure

👎 MNCs may pay low wages
👎 May encourage over-specialisation
👎 Profit may not stay in the LEDC
👎 Environmental damage in the LEDC
👎 Tax revenues in the LEDC may be minimal

Worked example

target
B–A

Tariffs and quotas are two ways LEDCs can restrict free trade. Which **one** of these do you think is most likely to reduce imports to a LEDC and why? **(6 marks)**

A tariff is a tax on imports. As this makes a product more expensive, businesses might decide not to import it, but this depends on the size of the business because...

This is an extract from a student answer.

EXAM ALERT!

Fewer than three in twenty students got full marks for this question. You should analyse the options, develop your points and make sure your answer is balanced.

There is no right answer! You can argue that either tariffs or quotas are most likely to reduce imports to a LEDC and you need to make your own judgement.

This was a real exam question that a lot of students struggled with – **be prepared!**   ResultsPlus

Now try this

target
C–B

1 State **three** reasons for imposing trade restrictions.   **(3 marks)**

2 Explain **one** drawback to a LEDC of a multinational operating in their country.   **(3 marks)**

93

Other help for LEDCs

Although international trade can help to reduce poverty in LEDCs, more help is needed. You need to know what governments and other organisations can do to help.

The debt problem

LOAN REPAYMENTS

+

INTEREST PAYMENTS

=

HIGH OPPORTUNITY COST
e.g. schools, hospitals and other government services

This debt problem can be relieved if rich countries cancel or reduce the debt burden.

Other government help

Although reducing the debt of LEDCs will raise their living standards, other measures include:

- financial aid
- encouraging investment in LEDCs to help increase productivity
- limiting population growth so that resources are spread less thinly
- encouraging diversification so that LEDCs are not reliant on one major industry
- encouraging free trade.

Charity and non-governmental organisation (NGO) roles

- The WORLD BANK aims at reducing poverty. It lends money for capital projects, such as irrigation systems, in LEDCs.
- The WORLD TRADE ORGANISATION aims to promote free trade by persuading countries to abolish trade barriers. It polices free-trade agreements and helps to settle trading disputes.
- The FAIRTRADE FOUNDATION aims to raise the incomes of farmers in LEDCs by offering higher prices for their produce, e.g. coffee and cocoa. These more expensive products appeal to ethical consumers.
- Other CHARITIES, such as Oxfam and Christian Aid, use a number of methods to raise money that is given directly to people in LEDCs.

Worked example

target D-C

(a) Identify **one** method that governments could use to help the development of LEDCs.   **(1 mark)**

Cancelling debt.

target C-B

(b) For this method, explain how a LEDC might benefit.   **(3 marks)**

This will allow the LEDC to keep more of its tax receipts. The extra taxes could be spent on education. People in the country will have more skills, be able to earn more money and get out of poverty.

Other methods for (a) could be:
- encouraging diversity
- encouraging investment
- limiting population growth
- encouraging free trade
- lowering taxes.

In part (b) you need to include **three** linked strands that build the explanation with reference to the context.

Now try this

target B-A

1   Explain **one** reason why debt is a problem for LEDCs.   **(3 marks)**

2   Describe the role of the World Trade Organisation in reducing poverty in LEDCs.   **(4 marks)**

Exam skills 1

You will have 1 hour 30 minutes to complete the Unit 5 exam paper. The paper is worth 90 marks and there are three sections (Section A, B and C). The paper will contain multiple-choice, short- and extended-answer, data-response and scenario-based questions.

Using your knowledge of business assess

What is meant by the term

Multiple choice

Give, state and identify

Calculate

Outline

Describe

Question types

Assess

Discuss

Questions using diagrams

Choice questions

Explain

Context

When an exam question refers to a particular business, you need to answer the question in the CONTEXT of that business. This means that your answer must talk specifically about the business in the question.

To do this, you should think about:

☑ the products the business makes

☑ who the competitors are.

Understanding the question

Make sure that you read the questions and any other information carefully so you can understand what the question is asking you to do. Do you need to identify, explain, describe, discuss or assess something?

You should also look at the number of marks available and make sure you spend the appropriate amount of time on each question.

Worked example

In 2009, Premiership champions Manchester United FC increased its ticket prices. Tickets are now 50% more than in 2005. Despite this, the club fills its stadium each home game.

There are three parts to this question and all three parts refer to Manchester United. Make sure that you think about this football club when answering the questions. There are three different question types here:

- Multiple choice
- Identify
- Explain

Make sure you understand what you need to do for each question.

(a) The demand for Manchester United football tickets is price insensitive. This means that when the price is increased: Select **one** answer.   **(1 mark)**

A ☒ Revenue increases   B ☐ Profit decreases

C ☐ Demand increases   D ☐ Costs increase

(b) Identify **two** factors that might affect the price sensitivity of a season ticket.   **(2 marks)**

1 Necessity

2 Time period (success of club)

Other possible answers include:

- whether there are any substitutes for the ticket
- percentage of income spent on a ticket.

(c) Explain **one** benefit to a business such as Manchester United of the demand for its tickets being price insensitive.   **(3 marks)**

As other football teams are not suitable substitutes for Manchester United fans they are willing to pay higher prices for tickets. So when the price of a ticket increases the demand does not fall very much and Manchester United's revenue increases.

EXAM ALERT!

Three in ten students got all three marks for part **(c)**. You need to make three relevant points and refer specifically to Manchester United tickets.

This was a real exam question that a lot of students struggled with – **be prepared!**

ResultsPlus

Exam skills 2

In your exam you will have to answer six, eight and ten mark questions. These are called extended-writing questions. To answer an extended-writing question effectively you should:

☑ read the question and any other information carefully

☑ make sure you understand what the question is asking you to do (e.g. do you need to make a choice, discuss or assess something?)

☑ use appropriate business concepts and terms

☑ develop your answer and support it with appropriate examples

☑ refer to the context given in the question (if there is one)

☑ make sure your answer is balanced.

Some of these questions are based around evidence and will give you a specific CONTEXT. You need to make sure that you apply your answer to the given context when answering these questions.

Worked example

target A–A*

Pollution and the use of non-renewable resources are two drawbacks of economic growth.

(a) Which of these do you think is the more serious and why?   **(6 marks)**

I think that the use of non-renewable resources is more serious because when these resources are used they are gone forever and cannot be replaced…

However it depends if renewable resources can take the place of non-renewable resources which means that using up non-renewable resources is less serious…

This is an extract from a student answer.

In this extract, the student has chosen 'use of non-renewable resources' and has started to explain why this is more serious.

When answering this question you need to **either** refer to both pollution and non-renewable resources, and evaluate why you have chosen one **or** focus solely on one choice and provide analysis and balance around this method. Remember that there is no right answer to these questions but you need to make sure you justify your choice.

(b) Do you think that Portsmouth FC's revenue will increase as a result of reducing the price of its season tickets? Justify your answer.   **(6 marks)**

Portsmouth FC season tickets are likely to be price sensitive as the reduction in the price of tickets would be expected to lead to a greater change in quantity demanded (and therefore revenue)…

target A–A*

This is an extract from a student answer.

In this extract the student has thought about the **context** of the question – Portsmouth Football Club. This means that the beginning of their answer is focused appropriately on the reasons why revenue might increase if ticket prices decrease.

EXAM ALERT!

Fewer than four in ten students scored five or six marks for this question. Students who did well identified the likely price sensitivity of the Portsmouth FC tickets and analysed how the decrease in price would be expected to increase demand.

This was a real exam question that a lot of students struggled with – **be prepared!**   ResultsPlus

Exam skills 3

Some of the extended-writing questions in Sections B and C will be assessed for the quality of written communication (QWC). These questions are marked with an asterisk. When answering these questions you should make sure that:

☑ your answer is written to a high standard

☑ there are no errors in spelling, punctuation or grammar

☑ the quality of language is high

☑ your answer is clearly structured.

Worked example

* (a) Princess Yachts International plc sells 15% of the yachts to the USA. Assess the effects a strong pound might have on their profits. **(8 marks)**

> A strong pound means that customers in the USA will have to spend more dollars to buy the same amount of goods in pound sterling in the UK. As such, the yachts will be more expensive for USA customers. This might cause demand for exports to decrease, affecting Princess Yacht's revenue...

This asterisk means that your answer will also be assessed for QWC.

This is an extract from a student answer.

This asterisk means that your answer will also be assessed for QWC.

In this part of the student's answer, the student is considering what a strong pound means for exports and is beginning to link this to the company's revenue. Your answer must contain **analysis** and **evaluation**.

* (b) The social networking business, Bebo, was acquired in 2008 by media giant AOL in a takeover deal. Using the evidence and your knowledge of economics and business, assess the extent to which consumers of social networking sites and employees of a business like Bebo, will be disadvantaged by the takeover. **(10 marks)**

> The takeover will disadvantage customers because there will be less competition, which will lead to less choice for customers. This means that AOL might be able to act as a monopolist. However, AOL might invest more to make Bebo a better site and there are other social networking sites available so there is some competition. A disadvantage to employees is...

This is an extract from a student answer.

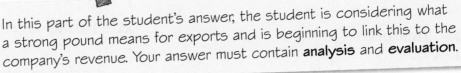

You must relate your answer to the given **context** to achieve high marks for this question. Your answer should have a clear, balanced view of the effects on consumers AND employees, and include the appropriate economics and business terminology, concepts and methods. You should finish with a well-supported conclusion.

Answers

Unit 1

The following pages contain answers to the 'Now try this' questions in Unit 1 of the Revision Guide.

1. Businesses
1 B

2. Understanding customer needs 1
1 C

3. Understanding customer needs 2
1 A

4. Market mapping
1 B and D

5. Competition
1 C and E

6. Added value 1
1 A and D

7. Added value 2
1 D

8. Franchising 1
1 A and E

9. Franchising 2
1 C and E

10. Enterprise
1 A and C

11. Thinking creatively
1 C

12. Questions entrepreneurs ask
1 B

13. Invention and innovation
1 B

14. Taking a calculated risk
1 B

15. Other important enterprise skills
1 D

16. Objectives when starting up
1 C, D, and E

17. Qualities shown by entrepreneurs
1 A and C

18. Revenues, costs and profits 1
1 (a) £7000
 (b) £5000
 (c) £5000
 (d) £7000

19. Revenues, costs and profits 2
1 C

20. Forecasting cash flows 1
1 B

21. Forecasting cash flows 2
1 A and E

22. The business plan
1 B and E

23. Obtaining finance 1
1 A and E

24. Obtaining finance 2
1 i c
  ii b
  iii d
  iv a

25. Customer focus
1 A and C

26. The marketing mix
1 C and E

27. Limited liability
1 D

28. Start-up legal and tax issues
1 B

29. Customer satisfaction
1 B

30. Recruiting, training and motivating
1 C

31. Market demand and supply
1 A

32. The impact of interest rates
1 B and D

33. Changes in exchange rates
1 C

34. The business cycle
1 A and D

35. Business decisions and stakeholders
1 D

37. Exam skills 2

1 i e
  ii d
  iii f
  iv g
  v h

Unit 3

The following pages contain suggested answers to the 'Now try this' questions in Unit 3 of the Revision Guide. In many cases, these are not the only correct answers.

39. Marketing

1 D

2 Marketing is the process of identifying and understanding customer needs in order to provide products and services that meet these needs profitably.

40. Market research

1 Market research is the process of gathering information about customers, competitors and market trends through primary or secondary sources.

2 Suggested answers include: questionnaires, surveys, tally count, observations, answers with a scale response.

3 Market research data will enable a company to find out how many people are interested in its product or might be willing to buy it. As a result the company can decide whether the product is appropriate for customers and if enough people will buy it to make a profit.

41. Product trial and repeat purchase

1 Product trial is a method used by businesses to persuade customers to try out a product for the first time. Consumers buy the goods and then decide whether or not they want to buy it again. If customers like a product when they first try it they are likely to make repeat purchases.

2 Customer loyalty is when customers continue to buy from the same business or buy the same product. If customers remain loyal to Pepsi Raw they will continue to make repeat purchases of the product in future. This will help to make the product successful and generate revenue. Customers may buy Pepsi Raw rather than other products by businesses such as Coca-Cola. This may help Pepsi to achieve its aim of catching up with its main rival.

42. Product life cycle 1

1 B

2 In the maturity phase, sales have peaked and sales growth will have slowed down. Launching a new product will be expensive. Using extension strategies may be a cheaper option. Changing the design of a product, for example, can give it a new lease of life. This may encourage existing and new customers to buy the product. The business may benefit from increased sales revenue.

43. Product life cycle 2

1 Product portfolio analysis allows a business to investigate the combination of products that it sells. It helps a business to make decisions about these combinations, such as when to launch products to, or remove products from the market.

2 Product portfolio analysis allows a business to manage the different products in its product mix. It allows it to see which products are doing well and which are not. It can then assess the revenue, costs and profit they are generating. As a result it can make decisions about whether products need to be launched or withdrawn or whether sales can be improved by advertising or other marketing methods.

44. Branding and differentiation

1 Suggested answers could include:
  - quality
  - unique name
  - packaging
  - customer service.

2 A strong brand might benefit a business because it will allow it to charge a premium price. As a result, it will receive a greater sales revenue. This will increase the probability a higher profits.

46. Successful marketing mix 2

1 D

2 A premium price is a price that is relatively high compared to the price of other rival products. Businesses often charge premium prices for high value, luxury, scarce or high-cost products.

3 A business might charge a premium price for its product because it is seen by customers as being a luxury good. Customers perceive the product as being of greater value or quality than other products. They will therefore be prepared to pay more for it. As a result, the business can earn high revenue from very few sales.

4 Effective promotion will boost customer awareness. This is likely to lead to an increase in product trials. As a result the product will move into the growth stage of the product life cycle. The sales of the product should grow and eventually make profits for the business.

47. Design and research development

1 Extended answer questions need to be well written, in sentences (not bullet points) and have a conclusion. Content could include:

- Cost is an important element of the design mix because Marks and Spencer's suits are not very expensive.
- M&S will need to keep its costs low in order to make a profit.
- The function of a machine-washable suit is fairly unique.
- This helps differentiate their product from that of competitors.
- Overall function is more important than cost as people are more likely to buy this suit for the functionality. (You might choose cost as being more important.)
- This will also depend on the appearance and style of the suit.

48. Managing stock 1

1 25 hamsters.

2 Just-in-time stock control is a stock system where stocks are delivered only when they are needed in the production system. No stocks are held by the business, so costs can be kept down and wastage minimised.

49. Managing stock 2

1 Stock is the raw materials, work in progress or finished goods that the business holds.

2 Holding stock is expensive. The more toys they stock the higher the costs and they will have to have somewhere to store all of the toys, which will cost money.

50. Managing quality

Achieving a high standard of quality will improve customer satisfaction. This will lead to repeat purchase and therefore increased sales revenue.

51. Cost-effective operations and competitiveness

1 Suggested answers could include:
- improving purchasing (cheaper suppliers)
- better design of products
- cheaper labour costs
- cutting overhead costs
- streamlining the production process
- relocation.

2 Extended answer questions need to be well written, in sentences (not bullet points) and have a conclusion.

Content could include:

- Increasing productivity will help McDonald's keep its prices low, which is important in the fast-food industry.
- The overall quality of fast-food will make it more desirable and this could add value.
- Improving quality is the most effective, especially as McDonald's sometimes has to battle with the image of its products being unhealthy. (You might choose improving productivity as being more important.)

52. Effective customer service

1 Customer service is the experience that customers have when dealing with a business. Effective service means meeting the needs of customers, spotting problems they have and solving them quickly and efficiently.

2 (a) Suggested answers could include:
- Poor customer satisfaction.
- Poor brand image.
- Inability to differentiate a product and gain a competitive advantage.
- Inability to charge a premium price.
- Fall in sales and profits. Sales changing to rival products.
- Fall in repeat purchase and customer loyalty.

(b) Poor customer satisfaction may mean that the customer takes a poor view of the experience they have had when buying from a business. They may not make repeat purchases of the product and may also discourage others from buying from a business. Sales and profits of the business could fall as customers chose to buy rival products.

53. Consumer protection laws

1 The Sale of Goods Act or the Trade Descriptions Act.

2 (a) Suggested answers could include:
- train staff on new legislation
- disruption to business
- financial costs of compliance.

(b) Some staff may be slow to learn or may not learn the new rules. As a result the business may not comply totally with the new legislation. It may fined, thus increasing its costs.

54. Improving cash flow

1 D

2 Suggested answers could include:
- reduce / slow down cash outflows
- build relationships with suppliers
- increase the level of stock the business can order without having to pay for it immediately.

55. Improve profit

1 Suggested answers could be insolvency, bankruptcy, lack of staff motivation or reduced investment.

2 Extended answer questions need to be well written, in sentences (not bullet points) and have a conclusion.

Content could include:

- £35 may be a better price to charge as this will help generate more revenue and increase the chances of making a profit in the first year
- the higher price will also help cover expensive start-up costs
- on the other hand, their business is new and London is a competitive market
- a price of £30 may make it easier to attract customers
- overall, the correct price may depend on the quality of their menu and if there are similar types of restaurant in the local area
- as their business in new, it is better to set the lower price. They can always increase prices to improve profit later, when the business has become established.

56. Break-even charts

1 The break-even point is the level of output where total revenue is equal to total costs. At this point the business makes neither a profit or a loss.

2 Profit = revenue − total costs

Revenue = quantity × price

Revenue = 20 000 × £300 = £6 000 000

Total costs = fixed costs + variable costs

Total costs = £2 400 000 + (£140 × 20 000) = £2 400 000 + £2 800 000 = £5 200 000

Profit = £6 000 000 − £5 200 000 = £800 000

57. Break-even analysis

1 Suggested answers could include:

- change in total revenue
- move away from the break-even point
- change in the margin of safety
- change in profit or loss.

2 A move away from the break-even point of the business means that the business would no longer break-even at the current level of sales. If prices fell, it would need to produce and sell more to break-even. The business would need to make sure that its customers would buy more products at the lower price and that costs did not increase, otherwise the business could make a loss.

58. Financing growth

1 Suggested answers could include:

- sale of assets
- retained profit
- owner's funds.

2 Retained profit is money that the business has made in previous years that remains within the business. Using this to fund growth means that the business does not have to pay interest as it would if it borrowed the money from a bank. So it is a relatively cheaper means of financing growth than external methods.

59. Organisational structure

1 Giving workers more responsibility further down the chain of command in a hierarchy.

2 A wide span of control can make it difficult for superiors to manage the workforce who are their immediate subordinates. This could lead to communication problems and therefore reduced performance and organisation of employees.

60. Motivation theory

1 Suggested answers could include:

- higher pay or bonuses
- respect from superiors
- chance to express yourself in your work
- increased job security
- friendships with work colleagues.

2 Improved motivation of the workforce could lead to the long-term commitment of employees. This means they are less likely to leave the company and this will help the business retain their best employees.

61. Communication

1 Suggested answers could include:

- jargon
- using inappropriate communication media
- cultural differences
- skills of sender or receiver
- feelings or behaviour of sender or receiver.

2 The using terms that are jargon can make communications difficult to understand. If the receiver does not understand the terms used they may misinterpret the messages. As a result the actions taken in response to the message may be incorrect, which may adversely affect a business.

62. Remuneration

1 A piece rate system will encourage manual workers to work harder and produce more units per hour. This will lower the average cost of production and lead to a greater profit margin on each product sold.

2 Extended answer questions need to be well written, in sentences (not bullet points) and have a conclusion.

Content could include:

- Increasing wages is an important aspect of motivating low-skilled workers as this will help them achieve their physiological needs.
- If there a few other opportunities for promotion or reward it is also important to motivate them through higher comparable wages.
- On the other hand, wages are unlikely to help employees achieve their higher order needs, which can only be achieved through self-esteem and opportunities to further their careers.
- Overall the importance of wage rates will depend on the industry and nature of the job.
- It is more important to increase wages if other competitors have higher wage rates.
- Ultimately wage rates is only one factor in achieving employee motivation and other issues, such as fringe benefits and promotion opportunities, should also be considered.

63. Ethics in business

1 Suggested answers could include:
- lobbying
- protests.

2 Suggested answers could include:
- add value
- source of product differentation
- gives a USP
- focus on market segment
- improved reputation and customer loyalty
- established brand
- motivated workers.

64. Environmental issues

1 Suggested answers could include:
- noise pollution
- air pollution
- traffic congestion
- resource depletion.

2 A business could use recycled packaging with its products. This would reduce the amount of waste going to landfill sites and therefore, encourage households to do the same.

65. Economic issues affecting international trade

1 A tax put on goods imported into a country which makes them more expensive for buyers.

2 Measures that reduce the price of goods sold abroad encouraging firms to export.

66. The Government and the EU

1 Suggested answers could include:
- health and safety regulations
- maternity and paternity rights
- accounting regulations.

2 Being part of the EU encourages free trade between countries. This means that UK businesses can export their products abroad without any taxes imposed. As a result, opportunities for expansion and growth are created.

Unit 5

The following pages contain suggested answers to the 'Now try this' questions in Unit 5 of the Revision Guide. In many cases, these are not the only correct answers.

70. Trade-offs

1 When choosing between different alternatives, sacrifices have to be made. In this case, by choosing to spend £5000 on a new van, Colin has sacrificed spending the money on a part-time office assistant. This is a trade-off that Colin must accept when making his choice.

Other answers could be a new hydraulic lift or a radio advert.

2 Opportunity cost is the benefit lost from the next best alternative when making a choice. In this case, the opportunity cost to Colin when choosing the new van is the benefit lost from employing a part-time office assistant. According to Colin's list of preferences this was the next best alternative.

71. Raising and lowering prices

1 Chocolate bars are price sensitive because they are all very close substitutes for each other. Consumers can easily substitute one brand of chocolate bar for another. So if the price of one bar rises sharply they can easily switch to another.

2 As demand for chocolate bars is price sensitive, a price cut in one brand should result in a significant increase in demand. Therefore revenue is also likely to increase.

72. Stakeholders

1 A stakeholder is a group with an interest in the activities or performance of a business.

2 In this case, the local community is the stakeholder with the most influence. This is because the local community is concerned with the plans of Gerrard plc.

73. Hidden costs or benefits

1 Suggested answers could include:
   - traffic congestion
   - noise pollution
   - air pollution.

2 Traffic congestion would have led to a build-up of traffic in the local area. Local residents may have been delayed in their travels as a result. They may have been late for work or other appointments. This could have led to a lower productivity in other nearby businesses.

74. Measuring success

1 Suggested answers could include:
   - improved quality
   - patent
   - copyright
   - image
   - customer service
   - lower costs.

2 If a business is able to obtain a patent on a new invention, for example, it prevents other businesses from copying. This gives the firm a monopoly for a period of time. This will allow firms to dominate the market.

75. Causes of business failure

1 D

76. Problems faced by the economy 1

1 Rising costs might cause inflation because if costs rise businesses may have to increase prices to protect their profits. The increase in costs might be caused by increases in the cost of raw materials, wages, utilities or any other business expense.

2 If consumer confidence falls it means that they may fear losing their jobs or that their income might fall. As a result they may postpone or cancel non-essential spending. Spending on clothes may be considered non-essential because people can 'make-do' with their current clothing.

77. Problems faced by the economy 2

1 Unemployment is a term used to identify those people who are actively seeking work and are in receipt of Jobseeker's Allowance or other benefits.

2 There may be lower tax revenues received by government as a result of lower incomes, profits and spending. This puts pressure on the government to cut its spending on public services, such as schools and the health service. Society may suffer as a result from poorer education, health and other services. Other suggested answers could examine effects such as higher state benefits, increased crime, less enterprise or the need to cut prices.

78. Exchange rates 1

1 Factors that might cause the value of the exchange rate to change include the demand for imports, the demand for exports, interest rates or speculation by the financial markets.

2 If the value of the pound changes from £1 = $2 to £1 = $1.60, then its value has weakened. It has weakened because a pound can buy fewer dollars than before, $1.60 dollars compared to $2 previously. This means that more pounds are needed to exchange for the same amount of dollars after the change in the exchange rate.

79. Exchange rates 2

1 C

2 B

80. The government 1

1 The interest rate is the cost of borrowing money or the return received by savers.

2 Taxation is used to raise revenue to fund government spending, regulate demand in the economy and change people's behaviour.

81. The government 2

1 (a) Suggested answers could include:
   - increase taxes on alcohol
   - increased education
   - raising the minimum age of drinking or age limit to buy alcohol
   - banning 'happy hours'
   - changing licensing laws.

   (b) Higher taxes on alcohol are likely to increase the price of alcohol in outlets. This should help to reduce demand for alcohol which in turn should reduce consumption. Lower consumption might reduce the ill-effects of drinking too much.

82. How businesses grow

1 A

2 A business grows when it sells more output. Internal growth involves selling more output without taking over or merging with another business. External growth involves one business joining with another. They may join voluntarily through a merger, or one firm may buy the other.

83. Why businesses grow

2 Economies of scale will result in a fall in average costs to the firm. This will enable them to reduce the selling price of their product, which may give them an advantage over their rivals.

84. Monopoly power

1 A monopoly is a business with a market share of over 25%. It is a business that has influence over the market.

2 Suggested answers could include:

- They can lower prices because they can reduce costs by exploiting economies of scale.
- They can develop new products because monopolies have more resources and can get patents.
- They can reduce waste because they avoid duplication.
- They can earn higher returns for people who are shareholders.

85. Controlling big businesses

1 A pressure group is an organisation that aims to influence the decisions of business, government and individuals, using tactics such as boycotts and protests.

2 Pressure groups try to influence the decisions of businesses to prevent consumers being exploited. A pressure group's tactics might influence the behaviour of the business's consumers. Consumers may boycott products. The business may reduce its prices to prevent the loss of sales and profits as a result of the boycott.

86. Growth

1 D

2 If a business invests in machinery, productivity is likely to rise. This is because new machinery tends to be more efficient. As a result more goods can be produced, leading to economic growth.

87. Growth and standard of living

1 The standard of living refers to the amount of goods and services a person can buy with their income in a year.

2 One problem with using GDP per capita as a measure of living standards is that GDP is an average value. It does not take into account the fact that the incomes of some people in a country may actually fall, while a minority may rise sharply. A sharp rise in a minority will distort the average.

88. Can growth be bad?

1 Suggested answers could include:

- pollution
- resource depletion
- higher waste levels.

2 Higher waste levels may lead to increased costs of waste disposal. Businesses may pass on the costs to consumers in higher prices, pollute rivers or dump waste in an attempt to keep costs down.

89. Sustainable growth

1 Sustainable growth is an increase in GDP that minimises negative externalities faced by future generations.

2 Suggested answers could include:

- trying to meet meeting the needs of a wider group of stakeholders
- adopting ethical codes of practice, such as refusing to deal with firms that sell guns
- carrying out corporate social responsibility audits, where firms asses their impact on society and the environment
- using renewable resources.

90. Government action

1 Suggested answers could include:

- raising prices
- improving efficiency in other areas
- developing new products that are more sustainable.

2 Regulation is one approach used by governments to reduce pollution. It is a 'softer' approach to controlling businesses and involves using rules, guidelines and codes of practice to minimise pollution. For example, in agriculture there is a code of practice for the handling and storage of fertiliser. This is designed to reduce water pollution. Many regulations are drawn up by specific industries and are monitored by officials appointed by the industry.

This self-regulation is criticised by some who say that there is too much self interest. These people argue that firmer measures are required such as legislation or taxation. Businesses cannot 'escape' from these measures and therefore they are more effective. I agree with this view. I think that some big businesses are too powerful and cannot be trusted to regulate themselves. Sustainable growth cannot be achieved without direct government intervention.

91. Is everybody equal?

1 Suggested answers could include:

- very low GDP per capita
- a lack of food, shelter, clothes and water
- low life expectancy
- low literacy levels
- poor infrastructure
- poor health
- high population growth.

2 Extended answer questions need to be well written, in sentences (not bullet points) and have a conclusion.

Content could include:

Better education for the poor gives them the ability to gain qualifications and become more productive. This makes them more attractive to an employer, so gaining a higher standard of living and making a contribution towards economic growth.

92. International trade 1

1 International trade is when countries import and export goods and services with each other. It is the buying and selling of goods or services between countries. For example, the UK could buy cars from the USA or sell banking services to the USA.

2 The Single European Market is an example of a trading bloc where all trading restrictions are removed. This encourages more trade between nations. As a result firms' costs may have fallen as they benefit from economies of scale and lower costs should result in lower prices and higher living standards for consumers.

93. International trade 2

1 Suggested answers could include:
- protect jobs in domestic industries
- protect infant industries
- prevent the dumping of cheap goods on the domestic market
- raise revenue from tariffs
- prevent the entry of undesirable goods.

2 When a multinational operates in a LEDC it is often expected that new jobs will be created. However, sometimes the new jobs are very low paid. As a result the incomes of people in LEDCs do not rise by as much as was expected. This has led to allegations that multinationals are exploiting workers in poor countries.

94. Other help for LEDCs

1 A heavy debt burden can prevent a LEDC from developing. This is because the loans have to be repaid plus interest. The opportunity cost of these repayments can be high because the money could have been used to invest in education and healthcare. Such investment would help raise living standards and stimulate growth.

2 The World Trade Organisation aims to promote free trade by persuading countries to abolish trade barriers such as tariffs and quotas. It polices free trade agreements and helps to settle trading disputes. However, it is sometimes criticised for being undemocratic and favouring wealthy nations over poorer ones.

Your own notes

Your own notes

Your own notes

Your own notes

Published by Pearson Education Limited, 80 Strand, London, WC2R 0RL

www.pearsonschoolsandfecolleges.co.uk

Copies of official specifications for all Edexcel qualifications may be found on the Edexcel website:
www.edexcel.com

Text and original illustrations © Pearson Education Limited 2012
Edited and contributions by Dave Gray
Edited and produced by Wearset Ltd., Boldon, Tyne and Wear
Typeset and illustrated by HL Studios, Witney, Oxfordshire
Cover illustration by Miriam Sturdee

The rights of Rob Jones and Andrew Redfern to be identified as authors of this work have been asserted by them
in accordance with the Copyright, Designs and Patents Act 1988.

First published 2012

16
10

British Library Cataloguing in Publication Data
A catalogue record for this book is available from the British Library

ISBN 978 1 446 90373 5

Printed in Slovakia by Neografia

Acknowledgements
The author and publisher would like to thank the following individuals and organisations for permission to
reproduce photographs:

(Key: b-bottom; c-centre; l-left; r-right; t-top)

Alamy Images: Alistair Laming 46, Jeffrey Blackler 81r, Johnny Greig 64; **Corbis:** Mast Irham / epa 63; **Getty
Images:** Andreas Pollok / Taxi 61r, Scott Olsen 49r, Sergio Dionisio 29; **Shutterstock.com:** 1000 words 77,
claudiofichera 50, Gorilla 87l, Guido Vrola 89, Losevsky Pavel 49l, Monkey Business Images 59, 87r, Sirozha
32l, Stephen Finn 81l, Yuri Arcurs 61l

All other images © Pearson Education

Every effort has been made to contact copyright holders of material reproduced in this book. Any omissions will
be rectified in subsequent printings if notice is given to the publishers.

In the writing of this book, no Edexcel examiners authored sections relevant to examination papers for which they
have responsibility.